24

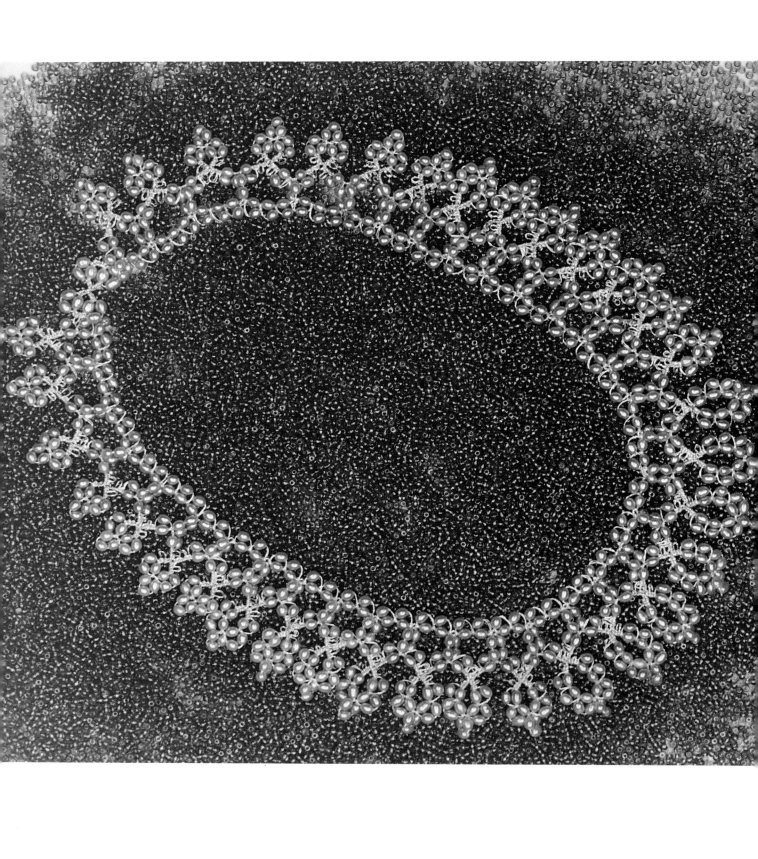

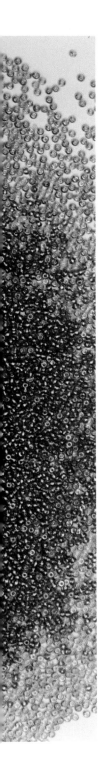

Tatted
Lace *of Beads*
The Techniques *of*
BEANILE
LACE

by

Nina LIBIN

Photography
Valeriy Libin

Book Design & Graphics
Nikolay Cherny

LACIS
Berkeley, California

Published by

LACIS
Publications
3163 Adeline Street
Berkeley, CA 94703
USA

ISBN 0-916896-93-5

Front cover: *Beanile motifs arranged into a flower,*
(a composition by Nikolay Cherny)

Back cover: *Pieces of Beanile lace.*
(a composition by Nikolay Cherny)

Title page: *Summer Necklace #2 worked in*
silver thread and fresh-water pearls
(for details see project **2.1d**, page 39).

preface and *acknowledgements*

For decades I was professionally involved in reviving the arts of
ancient needlework: crochet, hand-weaving, knitting, beadwork.
The whole rekindling process used to be extremely interesting
from looking for sources, mastering, adapting or updating the
researched needlework, to teaching it and writing about it.
In 1982 I came across tatting. For a while it replaced my profound
interest in bobbin lace, knitting, and hand weaving, but failed to
outshine beadwork.
Being unable to make a choice, I had to combine beads and tatting.
The simplest technique of stringing beads and tatting with this
thread works remarkably well. Beads and knots complement each
other immensely, merging naturally into a composite, which can be
defined as beadwork in lace format.
In 1988, in the very first publication, this lacy beadwork or beaded
lace was named *BEANILE* for "beadwork by Nina Libin"; to give
it a personal touch, and for the lack of a shorter term.

I am grateful to Jules and Kaethe Kliot for being encouraging and
enthusiastic about my work and sincerely hope the book will meet
their expectations.
Thank you Karey Solomon of Tatting Times, and my dear cousin
Faye Altman for reading the manuscript and making tons of
helpful suggestions at a very short notice.
I would like to thank the staff of The Image Photo USA Inc. for
their efficiency and friendly attitude.
Thank you, Nickolay and Vladimir Chernyayev, I really appreciate
your hand-made diagrams and line drawings; they are beautiful
and prove much quicker to tat than to draw.
This book would not be possible without the great patience and
unconditional support of my entire family.
And the last but not least, my greatest thanks are to my husband
Valeriy Libin for the endless shootings of Beanile pieces
and still kind of liking it.

All the finished projects and samples in tatting and Beanile lace
have been designed for this book and tatted by the author.

Nina Libin

contents

introduction   8

part ONE   ***simply tatting*** *(projects)*   11

1.1   *rings only*   12
    a - *plain ring*   13
    b - *two rings with picots*   13
    c - *decorative ring or Josephine picot*   13

1.2   *rings & chains*   14
    a - *strip of rings and chains*   15
    b - *chains in, rings out...*   15
    c - *outlining chains*   15

1.3   *clovers*   16
    a - *border of clovers*   17
    b - *alternating clovers and single rings*   17

1.4   *flower scroll*   18

1.5   *triangle*   20

1.6   *square motif*   22

1.7   *snowflake*   24

1.8   *single chains*   26
    a - *meandering chains*
    b - *two meanders intertwined*

1.9   *joined chains*   28
    a - *an edge of joined chains*   29
    b - *double strip of joined chains*   29

1.10   *all-in-one*   30
    a - *elongated motif*   31
    b - *joined elongated motifs*   32

part TWO	**tatting with beads** (projects)	35
2.1	*just a border*	36
	a - *a strip for edging*	37
	b - *summer necklace #1*	38
	c - *round neckline*	38
	d - *summer necklace # 2*	40
2.2	*twofold fillet*	44
2.3	*bracelet*	50
2.4	*net of beads*	54
	a - *beaded net for a screen*	55
	b - *pocketbook / glass-case*	56
	c - *beaded purse*	60
	d - *draw-string beaded bag*	61
	e - *pointed trimming*	62
2.5	*star motif*	64
	a - *snowflake*	66
	b - *amulet pouch*	68
	c - *Hanukah-Gelt pouch # 1*	70
	d - *Hanukah-Gelt pouch # 2*	71
	e - *dream-catcher*	72
	f - *hat of beaded net*	74
	g - *"snow cover" screen*	75
part THREE	**filigree motifs**	79
3.1	*trefoil*	80
	a - *arranging trefoils*	81
	b - *evening bag*	82
3.2	*plant scrolls*	84
	a - *vine scroll*	85
	b - *decorative composition*	86
part FOUR	**the techniques** (basics - innovations - helpful tips)	89
farewell		104
glossary		106
bibliography		108

BEANILE LACE
is a composite of *beads* and *knots*.
BEADS are glass seed-beads and gem beads,
while *KNOTS* make lace.

I believe that beaded lace is a needlecraft
in its own right, and has to be recognized as such.

Tatted Lace of Beads
sums up twelve years of experience
in designing Beanile lace, years of teaching basic and advanced tatting,
combining beaded tatting with crochet and a variety of finishing techniques.

Parts ONE and TWO offer forty projects designed to help learn and master:
- simply tatting
and
- tatting with beads

Every chapter includes a key for the projects, written patterns,
step-by-step diagrams or photographs.
Projects in part TWO contain detailed instructions.

Part THREE
- filigree motifs
introduces threaded beads and tatted knots
composed as an exquisite art form rooted
in two traditional handicrafts.

The last part of the book
- the techniques
covers basic tatting,
innovations related to incorporating
beads into lace and a few
helpful tips.

Ornamental possibilities
of beads and knots are truly endless.
Combining them brings out the best in both
and grows into a new needlework,
which can be defined as lace of beads.

There are numerous ways to incorporate beads into lace.
Usually beads are applied as a kind of surface decoration:
- Stitching beads / pearls onto lace here and there, to accentuate the design.
- Tambouring seed-beads onto ready-made lace to outline the pattern.
- Intertwining beads in, while making lace.

The most traditional bead - thread technique is
stringing beads; this proves to be ideal for organizing them into needlework
such as bobbin lace, crochet, embroidery, knitting, netting or tatting.

Whatever the technique, beads for centuries hold their position
between fine jewelry and costume making.

It is amazing how a simple action
of putting *thread* through the hole in *bead* unfolds
as a variety of techniques, from a single string of beads
into the sparkling richness of bead-weaving
and further on into
the shimmering elegance
of Beanile lace.

Interconnected
Triangles in
Repeating
Pattern

simply tatting

This part of seventeen patterns
is arranged in ten mini chapters.
They cover
elementary knotting exercises,
then unfold as basic tatting,
which grows into advanced lace making.

The projects have been designed or adapted
to introduce *tatting*, as an enjoyable needlework
and as the basic technique for *Beanile lace.*

Let us first recollect, what is tatting?
And what makes it lace?

Just two simple elements:
- *double stitch or double knot*
- *and picots for decorating and joining.*

Tatting offers a fascinating
possibility to combine
these two units in lace design
with endlessly interesting results:
- Different number of double stitches
changes the size of a tatted piece.
- Thread color gives color to the project.
- Thread texture specifies tatting texture.
While picots, besides being functional,
emphasize delicate shape of tatted lace.

To think, we have a lot to express ourselves
working this old type of lace
in a variety of projects,
from small and not-so-small
friendly gifts
to the interior decoration
accessories and
high fashion.

1.1

rings only...

any cotton thread #3-5
work with
ONE shuttle

If you feel comfortable with
tatting, you may skip to
part TWO and start
tatting with beads.

The following patterns are only for practice to make sure
beginning tatters start working halves of a double stitch
separately followed by the complete double stitch as a
tatting unit.
Worked in numbers, or divided by picots, these stitches can
be arranged into rings of any size and configuration.
Approximately 50 rings or 500 double and single stitches
prove to be enough to feel at ease with one shuttle tatting.
The originals were tatted in Parisian Cotton.

key *to the projects:*

R	ring
1, 2, 3...	number of double stitches
–	picot (regular loop)
J	decorative ring, known as "Josephine Picot"
½	the first half of double stitch
/	shape & tighten

Start the project leaving about 3" for a tail.
Work the first ring; tighten it.
Make an over-hand knot at about 3" from the first ring,
and start the next ring as close to that over-hand knot as possible.*

*repeat each pattern at least ten times to acquire necessary skills.

Patterns :

1.1a - *PLAIN RING*

R: 10/

fig. 1.1 - 1

1.1b - *TWO RINGS*
with PICOTS

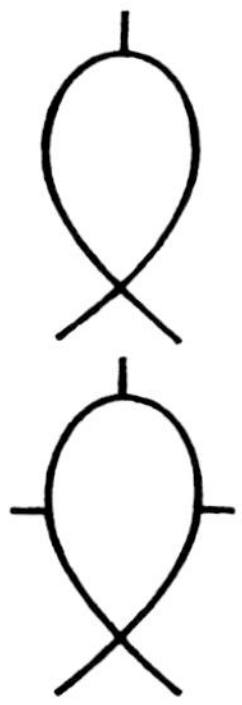

R1: 5 – 5/

R2: 4 – 4 – 4 – 4/

fig. 1.1 - 2

1.1c - *DECORATIVE RING*
also known as
"JOSEPHINE PICOT"

is a ring worked in the first
halves of the double stitch.

fig. 1.1 - 3

J: 12*
    *12 half-stitches to make a
     decorative "Josephine picot"

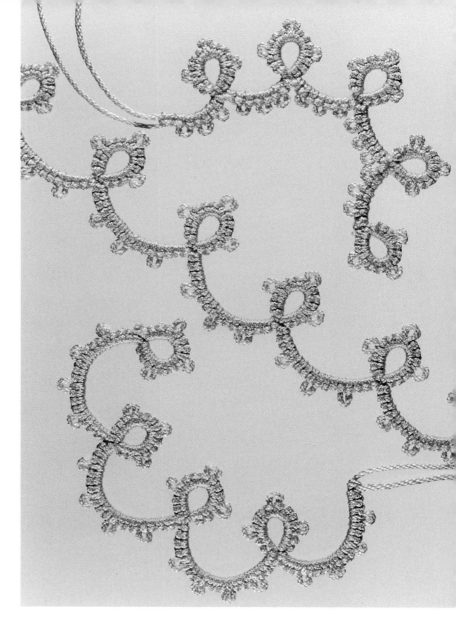

1.2
rings & chains

ONE shuttle and a ball
Continuous thread
Parisian Cotton

This chapter introduces:
chains,
working with continuous thread,
and *reversing the work,*
while switching
from ring to
chain.

```
_____ key _____ to the projects: _____

        R      ring
        CH     chain
     1, 2, 3...  number of double stitches
        –      picot
        /      shape & tighten
        //     shape, tighten & turn over
```

All the rings here have the same stitch count, while the
number of double stitches in chains is different in each
of three patterns.

Three patterns of alternating rings and chains
make simple edgings.

- Load the shuttle; do not cut the thread but leave it attached to ball.
- Start with a ring, when it is finished, turn it over.
- Wrap ball thread over your left hand, work chain.
- Chain done, turn it over (picots on the chain look down; the first ring is up).
- Work the second ring, tighten and turn it over.
- Pick up the ball thread for the second chain.
- Keep going for the needed length, working rings and chains alternately.
- Follow the patterns closely.

Patterns:

1.2a - *STRIPE of RINGS and CHAINS*

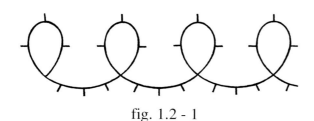

fig. 1.2 - 1

*R: 4 – 4 – 4 – 4//
CH: 4 – 4 – 4 – 4//

> *repeat from here, to make a border of ring/chain trimming.

1.2b - *CHAINS IN, RINGS OUT...*

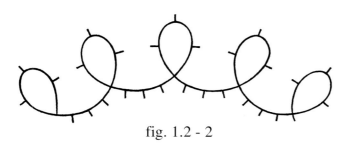

fig. 1.2 - 2

*R: 4 – 4 – 4 – 4//
CH: 2 – 2 – 2 – 2//

> *repeat from here, to make a curvy line with rings on the outside.

1.2c - *OUTLINING CHAINS*

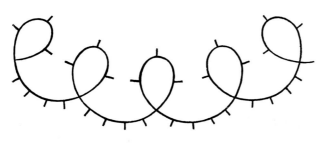

fig. 1.2 - 3

*R: 4 – 4 – 4 – 4//
CH: 4 – 4 – 4 – 4 – 4//

> *repeat from here, to make a trimming with rings looking inside.

Note: *the longer the chains, the closer the rings. The shorter chains push the rings apart.*

15

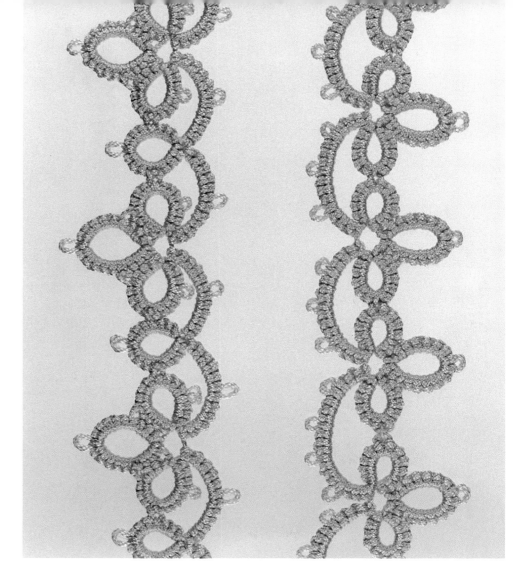

The two projects of this chapter introduce conventional (left side) joins.
In these patterns the ring you are tatting is joined to the previous ring – the one to the left.
These versatile edgings may be used to trim handkerchiefs, hems, cuffs and collars.
Two lengths of edging joined lengthwise by ring picots or chain picots make a rich and elegant insertion.

1.3

clovers

ONE shuttle & a ball
Continuous thread
Parisian Cotton

_____ *key*   *to the projects:* _____

R	ring
CH	chain
1, 2, 3...	number of double stitches
–	picot (regular loop)
+	joining
/	shape & tighten
//	shape, tighten & turn over

Patterns:

1.3a - *BORDER of CLOVERS*

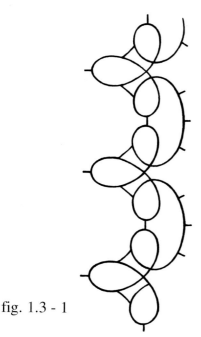

R1: 6 – 4 – 2/
R2: 2 + 6 – 6 – 2/
R3: 2 + 4 – 6//

      CH: 4 – 4 – 4 – 4//

*R1: 6 + 4 – 2/
R2: 2 + 6 – 6 – 2/
R3: 2 + 4 – 6//

      CH: 4 – 4 – 4 – 4//

*repeat from here to make a stripe of clovers.

fig. 1.3 - 1

1.3b -*ALTERNATING CLOVERS & SINGLE RINGS*

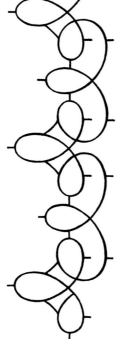

R1: 4 – 4 – 4 – 4/
R2: 4 + 6 – 6– 4/
R3: 4 + 4 – 4 – 4//

      CH: 6 – 6//

R: 4 + 4 – 4 – 4//

      CH: 6 – 6//

*R1: 4 – 4 + 4 – 4/
R2: 4 + 6 – 6 – 4/
R3: 4 + 4 – 4 – 4//

      CH: 6 – 6//

R: 4 + 4 – 4 – 4//

      CH: 6 – 6//

fig. 1.3 - 2

*repeat from here.
Clovers and single rings alternate with chains.

1.4

flower scroll

Rings & chains
TWO shuttles
Continuous thread
Parisian Cotton

In this chapter
we introduce
two-shuttle tatting,
the next step after
working with one shuttle
and a ball.

While *one* shuttle
is always used as a shuttle,
the second is mostly a ball.
However you will need
to switch shuttles to keep
the work flowing smoothly
(no twisted threads).

In the written instructions, the
point where the shuttles are
switched is marked (~).
In the diagram a solid line
indicates shuttle A; dashes
indicate shuttle B.

Another novelty here is
the final joining (^) which
uses the right-hand
shuttle to connect
the last two
elements
to each other.

	key	*to the project:*
	R	ring
	CH	chain
	1, 2, 3...	number of double stitches
	–	picot
	+	ordinary joining
	^	final joining
	~	switch the shuttles
	——	shuttle A
	-------	shuttle B
	/	shape & tighten
	//	shape, tighten & turn over

Pattern:

1) R: 4 – 4 – 4 – 4/
2) R: 4 + 5 – 5 – 4/
3) R: 4 + 4 – 2 – 2 – 4 – 4/
4) R: 4 + 5 – 5 – 4/
5) R: 4 + 4 – 4 – 4//

      6) CH: 4 +12//

7) R: 4 – 4/
8) R: 5 – 5//~

Important!

To follow the pattern, note where shuttles are switched on the diagram and in the written pattern. B will be your right-hand shuttle, while working ring 9, chain 10 and ring 11. After that switch the shuttles back for ring 12, chain 13, rings 14 and 15. The shuttles are reversed once again, to work ring 16 and chain 17, and switched back for rings 18 and 19.

    9) R: 5 – 3 – 4 – 4//

      10) CH: 4 ^ 14//

11) R: 3 – 4 – 4 – 3//~
12) R: 4 – 5 – 5 – 4//

      13) CH: 4 ^ 17//

14) R: 4 – 4/
15) R: 5 – 5//~
16) R: 7 – 7//

      17) CH: 20/~

18) R: 5 + 4 – 4 – 3/
19) R: 4 – 4/

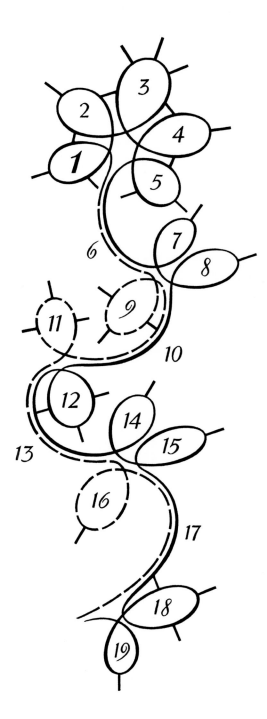

fig. 1.4 - 1

1.5

triangle

Two shuttles
DMC #10 Cébélia
Continuous
thread

This chapter features:

- Tatting with finer thread
- Rings on both sides
of a chain
- *Swirl joining* marked ⊕ in
written patterns.

In a design where
three or more
rings are joined at a single point,
there is no need
to make it a bulk of
multiple joins.
Instead, leave the first two
rings loose to be joined
with a single *swirl*
while tatting the last
of the central
rings.

key	*to the project:*
R	ring
CH	chain
1, 2, 3...	number of double stitches
–	picot
^	final joining
⊕	swirl joining
——	shuttle A
-------	shuttle B
~	switch the shuttles
/	shape & tighten
//	shape, tighten & turn over

Pattern:

TRIANGLE MOTIF for REPEATING DESIGN:

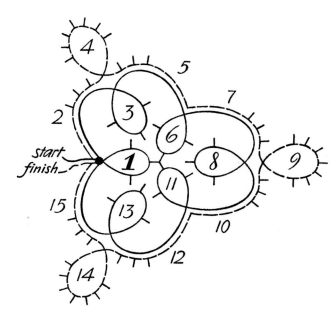

fig. 1.5 - 1

1) R: 6 – 3 – 3 – 6//

2) CH: 8 – 2 – 2 – 2/

3) R: 6 – 3 – 3 – 6//~

4) R: 6 – 2 – 2 – 2 – 2 – 2 – 2 – 6/~

5) CH: 2 – 2 – 2 – 8//

6) R: 6 – 3 – 3 – 6//

7) CH: 8 – 2 – 2 – 2/

8) R: 6 – 3 – 3 – 6//~

9) R: 6 – 2 – 2 – 2 – 2 – 2 – 2 – 6/~

10) CH: 8 – 2 – 2 – 2//

11) R: 6 – 3 ⊕ *3 – 6// *this *swirl* is one
of two joins
in the pattern.

12) CH: 8 – 2 – 2 – 2/

13) R: 6 – 3 – 3 – 6/~

14) R: 6 – 2 – 2 – 2 – 2 – 2 – 2 – 6/~

15) CH: 8 – 2 – 2 – 2/^
the final joining to the
base of ring 1.

1.6

square motif

Two shuttles
DMC #10 Cébélia
Continuous
Thread

Tat this motif to master:
rings on both sides
of a chain, and
multiple swirl joins.

The center
of the square is intentionally
dense to further explore the
possibilities of
the swirl joining.

All five joins in the pattern
are of the same
swirl type.

There are four triple swirls
and one quadruple swirl.
No ordinary joins.

key	*to the project:*
R	ring
CH	chain
1, 2, 3...	number of double stitches
–	picot
^	final joining
⊕	swirl joining
——	shuttle A
-------	shuttle B
~	switch the shuttles
/	shape & tighten
//	shape, tighten & turn over

Pattern:

SQUARE MOTIF for REPEATING DESIGN

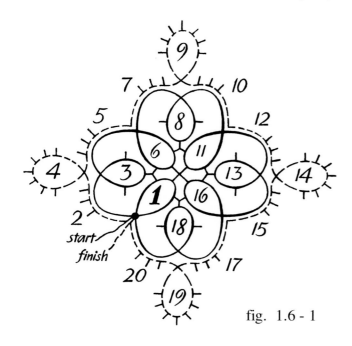

fig. 1.6 - 1

This chapter, like the previous and the following ones, is designed to encourage practice and develop ease with handling two shuttles and a continuous thread.

The basic goal is the same for all three projects: to produce single motifs, which may be joined by outer rings into repeating design.

If you like experimenting, try a different number of double stitches in those exterior rings. It will change size and configuration of negative space between the motifs.
As a result the fabric may look either denser or more open.

1) R: 6 – 3 – 3 – 6//

2) CH: 6 – 2 – 2 – 2/

3) R: 6 – 3 – 3 – 6//~

4) R: 6 – 2 – 2 – 2 – 2 – 2 – 2 – 6/~

5) CH: 2 – 2 – 2 – 6//

6) R: 6 ⊕ 3 – 3 – 6//

7) CH: 6 – 2 – 2 – 2/

8) R: 6 – 3 – 3 – 6//~

9) R: 6 – 2 – 2 – 2 – 2 – 2 – 2 – 6/~

10) CH: 2 – 2 – 2 – 6//

11) R: 6 ⊕ 3 – 3 – 6//

12) CH: 6 – 2 – 2 – 2/

13) R: 6 – 3 – 3 – 6//~

14) R: 6 – 2 – 2 – 2 – 2 – 2 – 2 – 6/~

15) CH: 2 – 2 – 2 – 6//

16) R: 6 ⊕ 3 ⊕* 3 – 6//

17) CH: 6 – 2 – 2 – 2/

   * this is a quadruple swirl
      join of rings: 1, 6, 11, 16.

18) R: 6 – 3 ⊕ 3 – 6//~

19) R: 6 – 2 – 2 – 2 – 2 – 2 – 2 – 6/~

20) CH: 2 – 2 – 2 – 2/^ final
      joining to the base of ring 1.

1.7

snow - flake

Two shuttles
Continuous thread

The original
Snowflake for Karey
was worked
in Parisian Cotton.

It seems to prove that even
a very thick thread can
look delicate when used
with the right
design.

No swirl joins here.
The six inner rings connected
by side picots make an
ornament with an
open center.

key *to the project:*

R	ring
CH	chain
1, 2, 3...	number of double stitches
–	picot
+	ordinary joining
^	final joining
——	shuttle A
-------	shuttle B
~	switch the shuttles
/	shape & tighten
//	shape, tighten & turn over

Pattern:

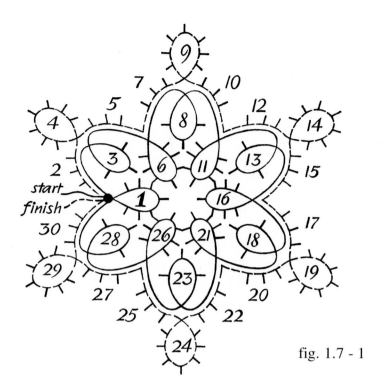

fig. 1.7 - 1

1) R: 2 – 2 – 2 – 2 – 2 – 2 – 2 – 2//

2) CH: 6 – 2 – 2 – 2/

3) R: 4 – 4 – 4 – 4/~

4) R: 2 – 2 – 2 – 2 – 2 – 2 – 2 – 2 /~

5) CH: 2 – 2 – 2 – 6//

6) R: 2 – 2 – 2 + 2 – 2 – 2 – 2 – 2//

7) CH: 6 – 2 – 2 – 2//

8) R: 4 – 4 – 4 – 4/~

9) R: 2 – 2 – 2 – 2 – 2 – 2 – 2 – 2/~

10) CH: 2 – 2 – 2 – 6//

Repeat positions 6-10 three more times. It covers positions 11-25 and brings us to:

26) R: 2 – 2 – 2 + 2 – 2 +* 2 – 2 – 2//

27) CH: 6 – 2 – 2 – 2/

*this joining is to the
first of central rings.

28) R: 4 – 4 – 4 – 4/~

29) R: 2 – 2 – 2 – 2 – 2 – 2 – 2 – 2/~

30) CH: 2 – 2 – 2 – 6/^ final
joining to the base of ring 1.

1.8

single chains

Two shuttles – two colors
Parisian Cotton or
Cotton thread #5

All chains - no joining!
Just alternating shuttles.

Each shuttle is wound
with a different-color thread
for clear resplendent tatting.

key *to the projects:*

CH	chain
2, 4, 6...	number of double stitches
–	picot
——	shuttle A
-------	shuttle B
~	switch the shuttles
/	shape & tighten
//	shape, tighten & turn over

Patterns :

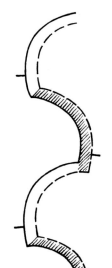

fig. 1.8 - 1

1.8a - *MEANDERING CHAINS*

- Wind two shuttles with different-color thread.
- Tie the tails.
- Start working on the first chain with shuttle A.
- Shape the first chain.
- Switch the shuttles.
- Work the second chain with shuttle B.

   A)   CH: 10 – 2//~
   B)   CH: 10 – 2//~
   A) *CH: 10 – 2//~   *repeat from here to make
                                      a meandering stripe
                                      in two colors.

fig. 1.8 - 2

1.8b - *TWO MEANDERS INTERTWINED*

- Wind two shuttles
  with a continuous thread of one color.
- Work a meander, switching the shuttles, as shown:

   A)   CH: 5 – 5//~
   B)   CH: 5 – 5//~
   A) *CH: 5 – 5//~   *repeat from here
                                  to make a meander.

- Wind two shuttles with a continuous thread
  of a contrasting color.
- Follow the same pattern.
- Tat a similar meander switching the shuttles
  after every chain.
- Make sure there is the same number of chains in
  both meanders.
- Adjust the picots; steam the pieces into shape.
- Intertwine them.
- No need for joining or twisting.

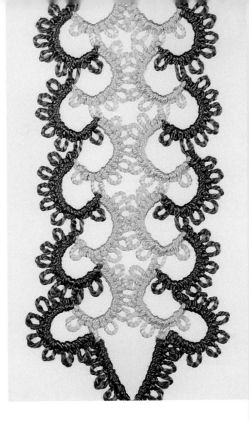

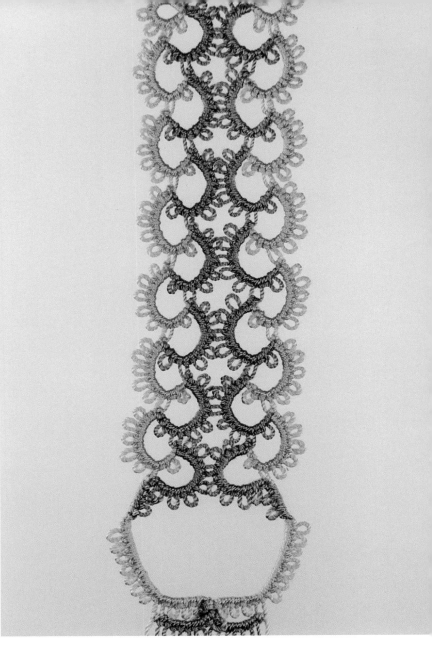

1.9

joined chains

Two shuttles - two colors
DMC #10 Cébélia
All CHAINS

Here are other ways
to enjoy *All Chains* pattern –
as an edging,
as a fabric or
as an exquisite bookmark,
when made in a short piece
and finished with a small tassel
or a lacy pendant.

(For a pendant patterns
see patterns 1.5, 1.6,
1.7, or 1.10)

key *to the projects:*

R	ring
CH	chain
1, 2, 3...	number of double stitches
–	picot
+	ordinary joining
^	final joining
——	shuttle A
-------	shuttle B
~	switch the shuttles
/	shape & tighten
//	shape, tighten & turn over

Patterns :

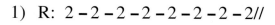

1.9a - *AN EDGE of JOINED CHAINS*

1) R: 2 – 2 – 2 – 2 – 2 – 2 – 2 – 2//

   Pick up another shuttle and use it as a ball.

2) CH: 2 – 2 – 2 – 2 – 2 – 2 – 2 – 2/^~

3) *CH: 2 – 2 – 2 – 2 – 2 – 2 – 2 – 2/^~

> * repeat from here and keep
>   switching shuttles
>   for every chain;
>   you will make a beautiful
>   lacy stripe.

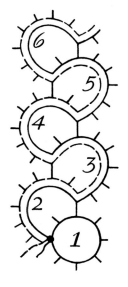

fig. 1.9 - 1

1.9b - *DOUBLE STRIPE of JOINED CHAINS*

ONE: 1) R: 2 – 2 – 2 – 2 – 2 – 2 – 2 – 2//

   Pick up another shuttle and use it as a ball.

2) CH: 2 – 2 – 2 – 2 – 2 – 2 – 2 – 2/^~

3) CH: 2 – 2 – 2 – 2 – 2 – 2 – 2 – 2/^~

Repeat positions 2) & 3) at least 10 times;
cut the thread.

Start another stripe similar to one you've just
tatted.

TWO: 1) R: 2 – 2 – 2 – 2 – 2 – 2 – 2 – 2//

   Pick up another shuttle and use it as a ball.

2) CH: 2 – 2 – 2 + 2 – 2 – 2 – 2 – 2/^~

To join hold the first stripe ring down
(fig. 1.9 - 2).

3) CH: 2 – 2 – 2 – 2 – 2 – 2 – 2 – 2 /^~

Repeat positions 2) & 3) at least 10 times, or
until both stripes are connected.

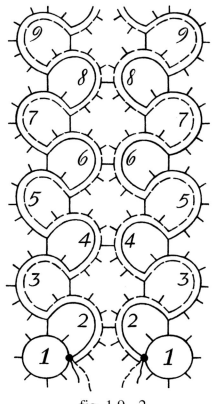

fig. 1.9 - 2

1.10

all-in-one

Two shuttles
Two colors
DMC #10 Cébélia

This elongated medallion
was designed to use all the tatting
skills developed so far.

- *Two motifs*
connected by tops make an
intricate bookmark.

- *Numerous motifs*
joined in a similar way become
an exquisite edging.

- *When attached side-by-side,*
they become a striking
clothing accessory – collar,
insertion, yoke,
short sleeve,
flounce.

key *to the project:*

R	ring
CH	chain
1, 2, 3...	number of double stitches
J	Josephine picot
–	picot
+	ordinary joining
^	final joining
⊕	swirl joining
——	shuttle A
-------	shuttle B
~	switch the shuttles
/	shape & tighten
//	shape, tighten & turn over

Pattern:

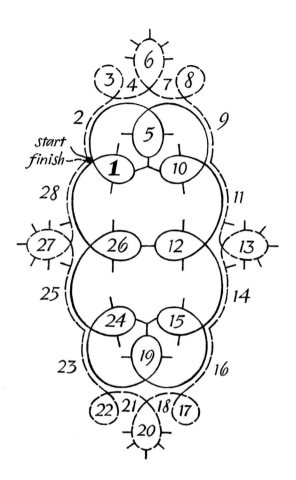

fig. 1.10 - 1

Originally, this pattern has been developed to combine numerous small things in basic tatting discussed in the previous nine chapters.

Besides, I cannot resist mentioning, that with lacy motifs, there are always quite a few possibilities of turning an abstract piece into something functional or into another "small gift" project.

1.10 - ELONGATED MOTIF

1) R: 4 – 4 – 4 – 4//
2) CH: 9~
3) J: 12/~
4) CH: 3//

5) R: 4 – 4 – 4 – 4//~
6) R: 4 – 2 – 2 – 2 – 2 – 4/~

7) CH: 3~
8) J: 12/~
9) CH: 9//
10) R: 4 – 4 ⊕* 4 – 4//
                *swirl joining to rings 1 and 5.

11) CH: 9 – 3//

12) R: 4 – 6 – 6 – 4//~
13) R: 4 – 2 – 2 – 2 – 2 – 4/~

14) CH: 3 – 9//

15) R: 4 – 4 – 4 – 4/
16) CH: 9/~
17) J: 12/~
18) CH: 3//

19) R: 4 – 4 – 4 – 4//~
20) R: 4 – 2 – 2 – 2 – 2 – 4/~

21) CH: 3/~
22) J: 12/~
23) CH: 9//
24) R: 4 – 4 ⊕* 4 – 4//
              *swirl joining to rings 15 and 19.

25) CH: 9 – 3//

26) R: 4 – 6 +* 6 – 4//~
              *ordinary joining to ring 12.

27) R: 4 – 2 – 2 – 2 – 2 – 4/~

28) CH: 3 – 9/^*
           *final joining to the base
           of ring 1. Tie and cut
           the tails off. Put the first
           finished motif aside.

fig. 1.10 - 2

To make a wide tatted strip of motifs for a collar (fig. 1.10 - 2) we have to join each motif side-by-side to the previous one. Start each new motif with ring 1:

1) R: 4 – 4 – 4 – 4//
2) CH: 9~
3) J: 12/~
4) CH: 3/~
5) R: 4 – 4 – 4 – 4//~
6) R: 4 – 2 – 2 – 2 – 2 – 4/~
7) CH: 3~
8) J: 12/~
9) CH: 9//
10) R: 4 – 4 ⊕* 4 – 4//

    *swirl joining to
      rings 1 and 5.

11) CH: 9 – 3//
12) R: 4 – 6 – 6 – 4//~
13) R: 4 – 2 – 2 +* 2 – 2 – 4/~

    *ordinary joining to
      ring 13 of the first
      motif (fig. 1.10 - 3).

14) CH: 3 – 9//
15) R: 4 – 4 – 4 – 4/
16) CH: 9/~
17) J: 12/~
18) CH: 3//   Continue following
                  the pattern
                  for the first motif.

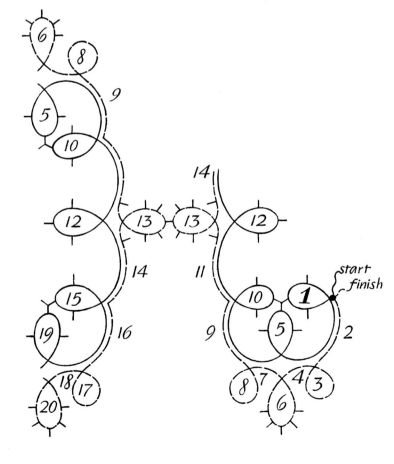

fig. 1.10 - 3

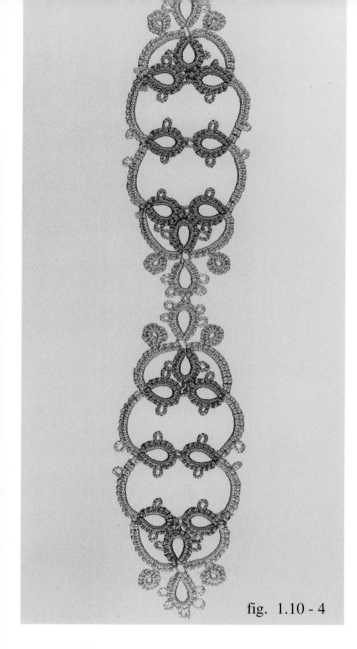

fig. 1.10 - 4

For a stripe of two medallions (fig. 1.10 - 4) work one finished motif and put it aside. Start the next piece with ring 1:

1) R: 4 – 4 – 4 – 4//

2) CH: 9~
3) J: 12/~
4) CH: 3/~

5) R: 4 – 4 – 4 – 4//~
6) R: 4 – 2 – 2 +* 2 – 2 – 4/~

   * ordinary joining to ring 20 of the first motif (fig. 1.10 - 5).

7) CH: 3~
8) J: 12/~
9) CH: 9//

Continue following the pattern for the first motif (page 31).

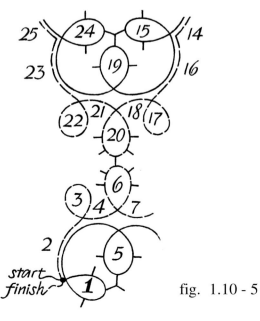

fig. 1.10 - 5

• *Needle the thread?*
　　- That's right, not the other way round.
• *Beads on ball thread,*
　　　though quite often there's no ball.
• *Beads on shuttle thread as well.*
　　　　- We do use a shuttle.
• *Beads up-&-down evenly.*
　　　　　- For "ribbon" effect.
• *Beads for intricate outline effect.*
　　　　- Oh, it's just an embellished picot.
• *Beads to maintain distance between tatted elements.*
　　　　　　- Very convenient and convincing.
• *Beads attached at the last moment.*
　　　- So, let them swing and dangle.

tatting with beads

A number of old and new techniques
may be used to combine beads and lace.

Stringing beads on one or more working threads
is a well-known, traditional way of incorporating
beads into textile.
It befits a number of needle arts including
embroidery, hand weaving,
knitting, crochet,
bobbin lace and tatting.

The following eighteen projects
present the basics of
tatting with beaded thread.
Most of the projects resemble (not repeat)
those in part One.
This similarity of the patterns
is intentional to show
how adding beads enriches tatted design.

We think it helpful to continue
providing every chapter with a short list of symbols
necessary to read the patterns in that particular chapter.

How-to and *Project-in-Progress* pages
are step-by-step instructions
related to a specific project
and placed next to it.

All the designs in this part are worked
in Parisian Cotton and 3-cut iris beads #9,
though any thread #3 or #5 will do.
The size of the thread is chosen to prevent beads
from either rolling off the thread
or getting in your way when not needed.

2.1

just a border

ONE shuttle & a ball
Thick cotton thread
3-cut Iris beads #9

The following four projects
have been specially designed
for this chapter
to introduce tatted lace of beads
known as *Beanile lace.*

They resemble those ring-chain
edgings in chapter 1.2, part One.

The familiar patterns should
leave us free to concentrate on
stringing beads and tatting this
beaded thread into
Lace of Beads
with beads on ball thread
and on shuttle thread as well.

The projects make
great necklaces and necklines,
edgings for collars,
a variety of curved or
linear trimmings,
to name just
a few.

key *to the projects:*

R	ring
CH	chain
1, 2, 3...	number of double knots
–	picot
+	regular joining
^	final joining
:	1 bead up & 1 bead down
···	pointed picot of 3 "up" beads
····	flat-top picot of 4 "up" beads
/	shape & tighten
//	shape, tighten & turn over

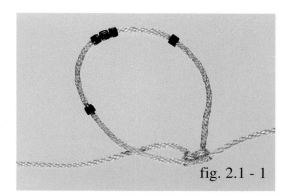

fig. 2.1 - 1

Very important!
Before starting any beaded ring, make sure you have on your loop the exact number of beads for that particular ring.
*For each ring of the projects **2.1a, 2.1b** and **2.1c** you will need **5** "up" beads on the loop (**3** of them for the pointed picot) plus **2** beads flanking the picot on both sides.*
2 "down" beads you will slide from the shuttle as needed.

Patterns:

2.1a - A STRIPE for EDGING

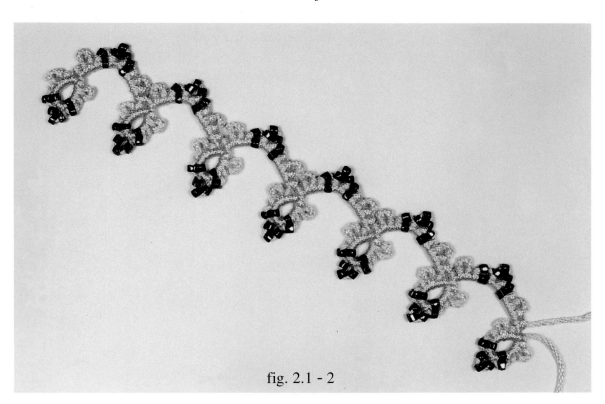

fig. 2.1 - 2

*R: 2 – 2 : 1 ⋯ 1 : 2 – 2//
CH: 2 – 2 : 1 ⋯ 1 : 2 – 2//

* repeat from here 6 more times to continue the pattern and complete the project with a ring.

2.1b - *SUMMER NECKLACE #1*

fig. 2.1 - 3

*R: 4 – 2 : 1 ⋯ 1 : 2 – 2//
CH: 2 – 2 : 1 ⋯ 1 : 2 – 2//

*repeat from here 34 more times,
    then complete the project with a ring.

2.1c - *ROUND NECKLINE*

fig. 2.1 - 4

*R: 2 – 2 : 1 ⋯ 1 : 2 – 2//
CH: 2 – 4 : 1 – 1 : 4 – 2//

*repeat from here as many times as you need to make
    a round or oval neckline; the original piece has thirty
    ring-chain modules plus a ring to finish the project.

fig. 2.1 - 5

• *OUTLINING RINGS*

Please, read the pattern and follow it closely for each of five stripes.
The chains are the same through the entire project but the number of beads in the rings varies.
The necklace starts and ends with the smallest rings in similar stripes 1 and 5.
The rings become larger in side portions 2 and 4 which are also alike.
The largest rings make central part 3.

1) *R: 2 – 2 : 1 ⋯ 1 : 2 – 2//
    CH: 2 – 2 : 1 ⋯⋯ 1 : 2 – 2//   *repeat from here six more times.

2) *R: 2 – 2 : 1 : 1 ⋯ 1 : 1 : 2 – 2//
    CH: 2 – 2 : 1 ⋯⋯ 1 : 2 – 2//   *repeat from here six more times.

3) *R: 2 – 2 : 1 : 1 : 1 ⋯ 1 : 1 : 1 : 2 – 2//
    CH: 2 – 2 : 1 ⋯⋯ 1 : 2 – 2 //   *repeat from here six more times.

4) *R: 2 – 2 : 1 : 1 ⋯ 1 : 1 : 2 – 2//
    CH: 2 – 2 : 1 ⋯⋯ 1 : 2 – 2//   *repeat from here six more times.

5) *R: 2 – 2 : 1 ⋯ 1 : 2 – 2//
    CH: 2 – 2 : 1 ⋯⋯ 1 : 2 – 2//   *repeat from here six more times.

Complete the project with R: 2 – 2 : 1 ⋯ 1 : 2 – 2//
All in all, there are 35 outlining rings interconnected by 34 chains.

•• *NECK-LINE CHAIN:*

CH: ^ 1 : : 1 : : 1 ~ 1 : 1 : 1 : 1 + 1 : 1 : 1 : 1 + 1 : 1 : 1 : 1 + 1...
Keep going, until all the chains are connected by neckline, complete with: ~ 1 : : 1 : : 1 ^
See *Project-in-Progress* (pp. 41- 43) for details and step-by-step instructions.

How to
work the projects starting from scratch:

- To start every project take a length (2 - 3 yards) of thread, fold it in half, and
  mark the center with a very loose over-hand knot.
- Needle both tails of each thread (see page 90).

Helpful: *Look at the photograph of a particular project to count the needed number of beads.*
Figure out how many "up" and "down" beads you will need for all the rings.
Count how many "down" beads are necessary for all the chains.
String the total number of beads on one needled tail, and load the shuttle with this half
of the thread.
The "up" beads for all the chains go on the opposite needled tail, which serves as a ball.

- For 7 rings and 6 chains of *A STRIPE for EDGING* (project **2.1a**) string **61** beads on one tail.
- Load this half of the thread on your shuttle.
- For those 6 chains string **30** beads on the ball tail, and leave it; no knot is necessary
  with this kind of thread, the beads will not fall off.

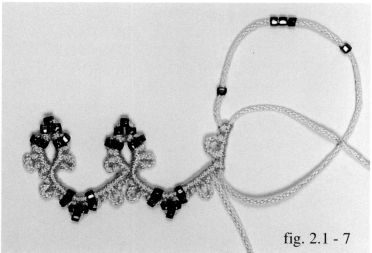

fig. 2.1 - 6   fig. 2.1 - 7

- For the *SUMMER NECKLACE #1* (project **2.1b**) string **315** beads for the shuttle
  and **180** beads for the ball.

- For the *ROUND NECKLINE* (project **2.1c**) string **270** beads for the shuttle
  and **150** beads for the ball.

- For the *SUMMER NECKLACE #2* (project **2.1d**) you will have to string **427** beads for
  the shuttle and **180** beads for the ball on 16-17 yards of thread, which may be difficult to
  handle. See *Project-in-Progress* (pages 41-43) for details and options for this particular project.

- Carefully read the patterns for every project, and follow them closely.
- After completing a project, stretch it on the table to be certain that everything is correct.
- If you have had to add thread, and there are loose tails, pull them all on one side; tie square
  knots and cut the tails off .
- The alternative is to split the 4-ply thread and hide the thinner threads separately.
- Adjust all the picots, beaded and plain, before steaming the work into shape.

Project-in-Progress:

*Notice: There are 34 similar chains and 35 rings of three different sizes, within the pattern **2.1d**. To work it in one piece we need 16-17 yards of thread with 607 beads on it.*

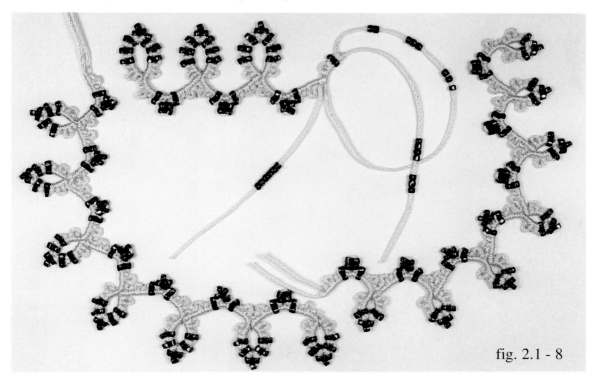

fig. 2.1 - 8

Working separately each portion of *SUMMER NECKLACE #2* seems the most convenient way.
- For the first and the last stripes take about three yards if you are working with thick thread.
- Mark the center, and needle the thread on both ends.
- Pre-string **42** beads on the 'ball' side and **49** beads for the shuttle.
- Wind the shuttle part of the thread onto the shuttle.
- Start with a ring R: 2 − 2 : 1 ⋯ 1 : 2 − 2//.
- Continue with a chain CH: 2 − 2 : 1 ⋯⋯ 1 : 2 − 2// (see the pattern and fig. 2.1 - 9).

fig. 2.1 - 9

After the first seven rings and seven chains are done, put the piece aside.
Take a longer thread, approximately 3.25 - 3.5 yards, and needle it on both ends.
- String **42** beads for the ball, and **77** beads for the shuttle.
- Load the shuttle, and start with the ring R: 2 − 2 : 1 : 1 ⋯ 1 : 1 : 2 − 2//.
- The rings in this stripe are larger and you will need 7 beads on the loop for every ring.
- The chains are the same CH: 2 − 2 : 1 ⋯⋯ 1 : 2 − 2// (see the pattern and fig. 2.1 - 10).

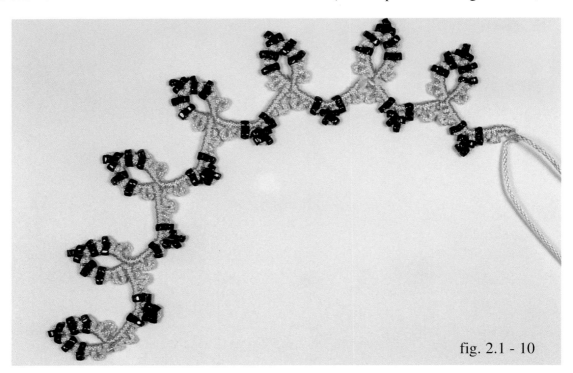

fig. 2.1 - 10

After completing this second stripe of rings and chains, put it aside.
Start the central part of the necklace (see the pattern and fig. 2.1 - 11).

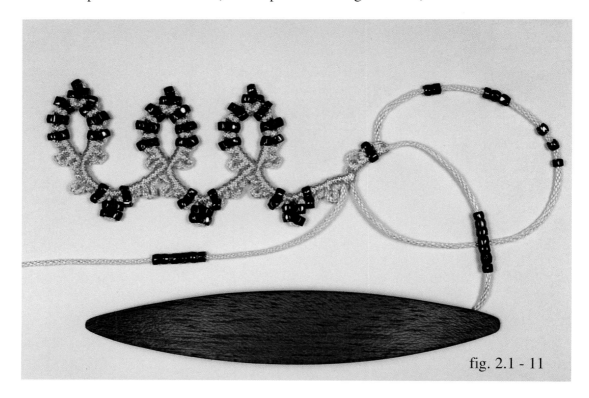

fig. 2.1 - 11

- Take about 4 yards of thread.
- Needle both tails, and pre-string **42** beads for the ball and **105** beads for the shuttle.
- Start with a ring: $2 - 2 : 1 : 1 : 1 \cdots 1 : 1 : 1 : 2 - 2//$ and finish the central stripe with a chain; the chains are the same: $2 - 2 : 1 \cdots 1 : 2 - 2//$ through the whole project.
- Put the finished central part aside, and switch to portion four; which is similar to the second stripe, starts also with a ring: $2 - 2 : 1 : 1 \cdots 1 : 1 : 2 - 2//$ and ends with a chain.
- Once the last 3 yards of thread are needled and beaded, start the end portion once again alternating rings: $2 - 2 : 1 \cdots 1 : 2 - 2//$ and chains: $2 - 2 : 1 \cdots 1 : 2 - 2//$.
- Complete this portion with the ring: $2 - 2 : 1 \cdots 1 : 2 - 2//$.
- Stretch 5 finished stripes and steam them into shape.
  Attach the last chain of stripe 1 to the base of the first ring in stripe 2 by final joining.
- The seventh chain of stripe 2 gets joined to the base of the first ring in central portion.
- The seventh chain of the central part goes to the base of the first ring in stripe 4.
- The seventh chain of stripe 4 must be joined to the base of the first ring in stripe 5 (fig. 2.1 - 8).
- String **113** beads for the ball and **113** beads for the shuttle on another thread-length.
- Twofold the thread and join it to the base of the first ring in stripe 1.
- Start the long chain of neckline assembling the necklace as you tat (fig. 2.1 – 12).

fig. 2.1 - 12

I would not recommend using an extremely long continuous thread with hundreds of beads, but if you feel comfortable working 5 yards of thread with about 200 beads, try making this necklace in 3 steps instead of 6, that is:
- Combine steps 1 and 2 of the pattern in one long stripe of 14 rings (7 small, 7 larger) and 14 equal chains.
- Work steps 3 and 4 as a stripe of 14 rings and 14 chains.
Please do not forget to check the number of beads before starting any of those rings.
- Tat the last portion of 7 rings and 6 chains, shape the necklace by working the neckline row.
- Pull all the tails on one side and join loose chains to the bases of proper rings.

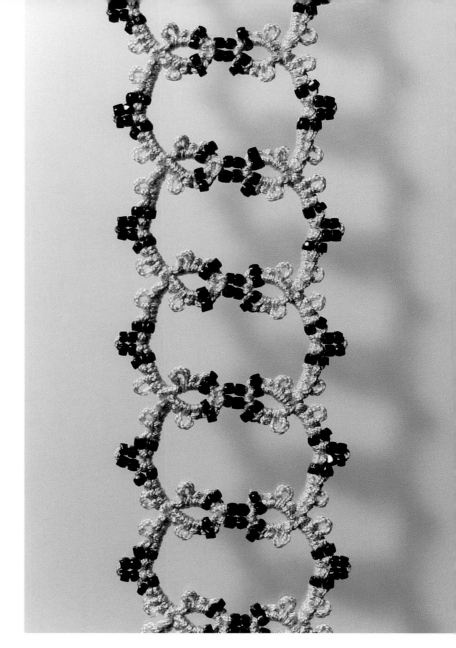

2.2

twofold fillet

ONE shuttle & a ball
Parisian Cotton thread
3-cut Iris beads #9

The double border of this chapter
is a ring-to-ring version
designed originally
for *a cuff*.

Repeated twice it became
a choker.

If worked denser and longer,
the band can be
a beaded belt.

The pattern is good
for very open
insertions.

key *to the project:*

R	ring
CH	chain
1, 2, 3...	number of double stitches
–	picot
:	1 bead up & 1 bead down
....	flat-top picot of 4 "up" beads
+	ordinary joining
^	final joining
~	switch the shuttles
/	shape & tighten
//	shape, tighten & turn over

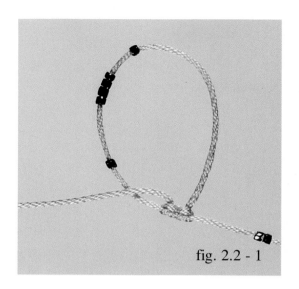

fig. 2.2 - 1

Very important:

Before starting any beaded ring make sure you have on your loop the exact number of beads for that particular ring!

In this case:
6 "up" beads on the loop, 4 of them for the long picot plus 2 beads for each side of that picot.
2 "down" beads you will slide from the shuttle, as needed (fig. 2.2 - 1).

Pattern:

ROW ONE (detail A):

*R: 2 − 2 : 1 ···· 1 : 2 − 2//
CH: 2 − 2 : 1 ···· 1 : 2 − 2//

> * repeat from here (fig. 2.2 - 2) until there are 7 rings and 6 chains.

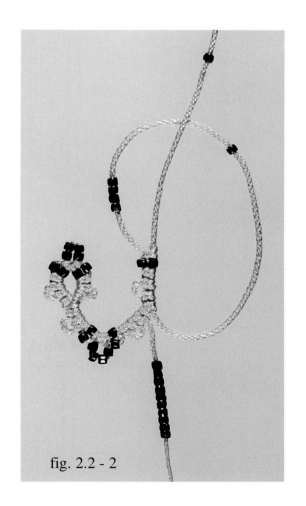

fig. 2.2 - 2

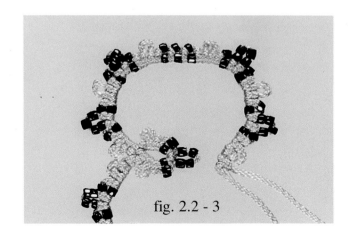

fig. 2.2 - 3

Now the pattern develops into a long U-turn chain (fig. 2.2 - 3)
CH: 2 − 2 : 1 ···· 1 : 2 − 2 : 1 ···· 1 : 2 − 2 : 1 : 1 : 2 − 2 : 1 ···· 1 : 2 − 2 : 1 ···· 1 : 2 − 2/

After you have completed detail A, there are 7 rings, 6 chains, and the U-turn chain.

Now shape the detail (fig. 2.2 - 4), and put it aside for a while; actually the whole project can be a continuous double border, but at this stage two shorter stripes seem easier to handle.

fig. 2.2 - 4

ROW TWO (detail B):

*R: 2 – 2 : 1 + 1 : 2 – 2 //
CH: 2 – 2 : 1 ···· 1 : 2 – 2//

*repeat from here joining detail B to detail A (fig. 2.2 - 5).

Be careful: although it is not technically difficult, connecting a ring to a beaded picot may seem tricky at first.
Pay special attention to the joining point and where you're putting the crochet hook.
Make sure there are only 2 "up" beads for every ring in this row.

See pages 48 - 49 for step-by-step instructions.

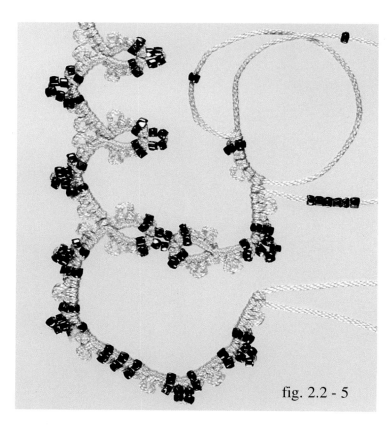

fig. 2.2 - 5

fig. 2.2 - 6

After you've completed the seventh ring of detail B, all the rings are joined, and the pattern develops into another U-turn chain similar to the long chain of detail A (fig. 2.2 - 6):

$$2 - 2 : 1 \cdots 1 : 2 - 2 : 1 \cdots 1 : 2 - 2 : 1 : 1 : 2 - 2 : 1 \cdots 1 : 2 - 2 : 1 \cdots 1 : 2 - 2/^\wedge$$

To finish the project, the two U-turn chains have to be joined to the first rings in every row (fig. 2.2 - 7).

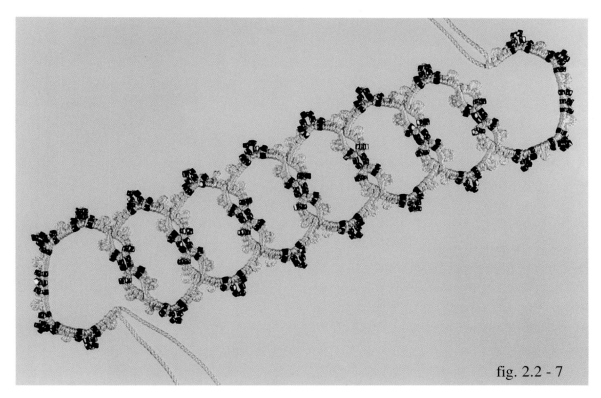

fig. 2.2 - 7

How to
make a double border starting from the very beginning:

- Take two lengths (about 6 yards) of Parisian Cotton or any cotton thread #3 or #5.
- Fold them in half and mark the center with a very loose over-hand knot.
- Needle both tails of each thread   (see page 90).

Helpful:

There are 7 rings + 6 chains + the long chain of U-turn in detail A;
the pattern indicates, that we need 6 "up" and 2 "down" beads for each ring and 2 "down" beads for every chain, + 11 "down" beads for the long U-turn chain, all of them should be on the same thread.
It means that we need (6 + 2) x 7 = 56 + (2 x 6) = 12 + 11 = 79 beads on the shuttle thread.

For *row ONE* (detail A):

- String **79** beads on one tail.
- Load this half of the thread on your
  shuttle.
- String **36** beads for those 6 chains
  plus **27** beads for the U-turn chain
  on the opposite tail of the thread,
  and leave it.
- Work detail A and put it aside.

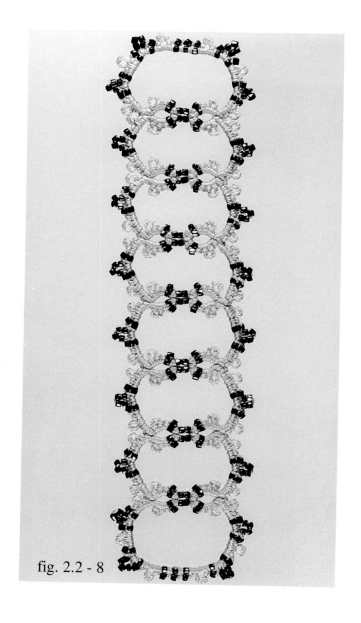

For *row TWO* (detail B):

- String **51** beads on one tail.
- Wind your shuttle with this thread.
- String **63** beads on the opposite tail and
  leave it; no knot is necessary.
- Work detail B following the pattern.
- Shape the second U-turn chain.
- Attach the U-turn chain of detail A to the
  base of the first ring in detail B.
- Attach the U-turn chain of detail B to the
  base of the first ring in detail A
  (fig. 2.2 - 8).
- Pull all the tails on one side.
- Tie square knots & cut the tails.
- Adjust the picots.
- Steam the band into shape.

fig. 2.2 - 8

Project-in-Progress:

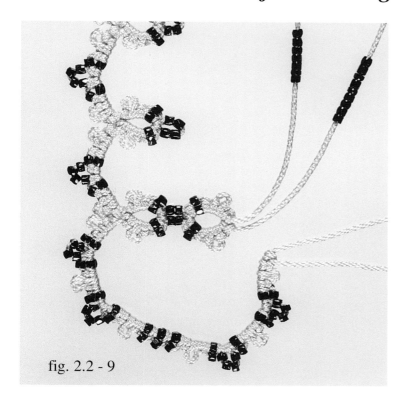

fig. 2.2 - 9

Start row TWO (detail B) with:
R: 2 – 2 : 1 + 1 : 2 – 2//

Be careful!

DO NOT FORGET TO HAVE 2 BEADS (instead of 6) ON THE LOOP FOR EVERY RING IN THIS ROW.

When you reach the joining point:
- Pick up detail A.
- Hold it U-turn chain down.
- Join by ordinary joining your
  current detail B to the beaded
  picot of the last ring
  in detail A (fig. 2.2 - 9).

Very important:

*BEFORE TIGHTENING THE FIRST RING OF DETAIL B, CHECK TWICE TO MAKE SURE YOU HAVE JOINED IT CORRECTLY,
THAT IS, TO THE LAST RING OF
DETAIL A, THE ONE CLOSEST TO THE COMPLETED U-TURN.*

Proceed with the first regular chain:
CH: 2 – 2 : 1 ···· 1 : 2 – 2//.
You will need only **2** beads on the loop for every ring in this row:
R: 2 – 2 : 1 + 1 : 2 – 2//
(fig. 2.2 - 10).

fig. 2.2 - 10

Note: If you feel comfortable handling 5-6 yards of beaded thread, you could work this project as one continuous pattern.

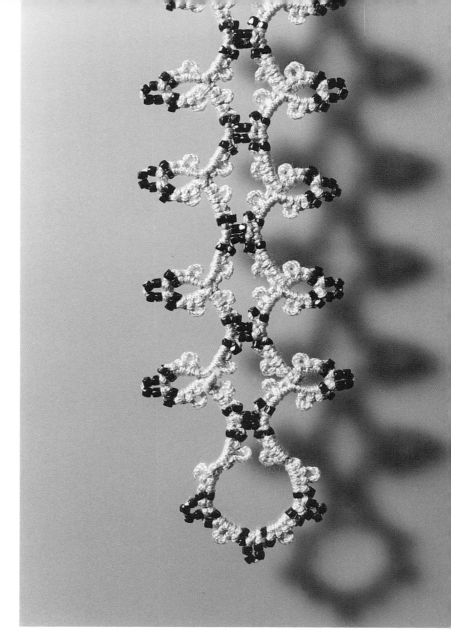

2.3
bracelet

TWO shuttles
Parisian Cotton thread
3-cut Iris beads #9

The project
in this chapter
is a chain-to-chain
version of a continuous double
border, designed for a bracelet.

The same twofold border may
become a cuff or neckwear,
reminiscent of medieval castles,
beautiful ladies in heavy silks
and precious cut-work.

That vision,
and the earliest understanding
of lace as both embellishing
and functional has been
greatly inspiring.

This pattern makes a stunning
lacy trimming or
insertion.

---

key   *to the project:*

R	ring
CH	chain
1, 2, 3...	number of double knots
–	picot
:	1 bead up & 1 bead down
....	flat-top picot of 4 "up" beads
+	ordinary joining
^	final joining
~	switch the shuttles
/	shape & tighten
//	shape, tighten & turn over

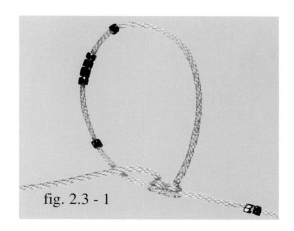

fig. 2.3 - 1

Reminder:

Before starting any beaded ring, make sure you have on your loop the exact number of beads for that particular ring!
In this case: **6** *"up" beads on the loop,*
4 *of them for the long picot*
plus **2** *side beads for each side of that picot;*
2 *"down" beads*
you will slide from the shuttle as needed (fig. 2.3 - 1).

Pattern:

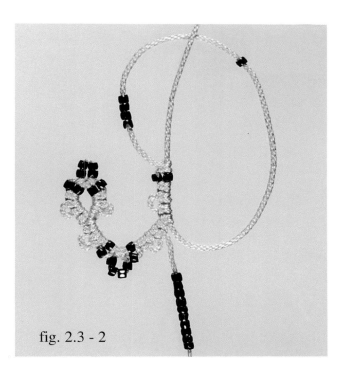

fig. 2.3 - 2

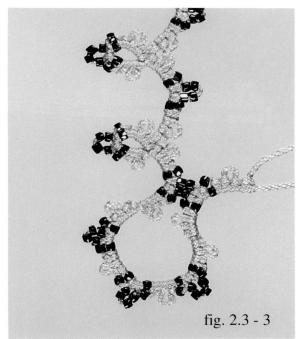

fig. 2.3 - 3

*R: 2 – 2 : 1 ···· 1 : 2 – 2//
CH: 2 – 2 : 1 ···· 1 : 2 – 2//

* repeat from here to continue the ring-chain pattern, which looks very much like the first row of the project **2.2** (fig. 2.3 - 2).

The similarity ends after the seventh ring is completed, and the pattern takes a U-turn.
It is a long chain of 3 portions different from the U-turn chain of the ring-to-ring border in the previous project; you will have to switch the shuttles after the first two portions:

CH: 2 – 2 : 1 ···· 1 : 2 – 2 /~
CH: 2 – 2 : 1 ···· 1 : 2 – 2 : 1 ···· 1 : 2 – 2 : 1 ···· 1 : 2 – 2 /~
CH: 2 – 2 : 1 +* 1 : 2 – 2//

* only **2** beads (instead of 6) are needed for every regular chain from here to the last regular chain of the project (fig. 2.3 - 3).

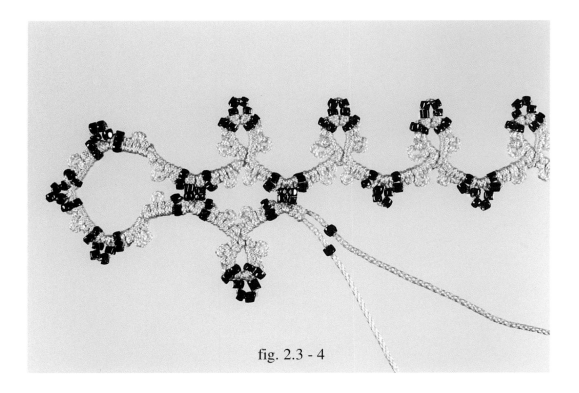

fig. 2.3 - 4

*R: 2 – 2 : 1 ···· 1 : 2 – 2 //
CH: 2 – 2 : 1 + 1 : 2 – 2//   *Repeat from here joining chains, as you keep tatting,
                                               while moving into the direction of the very first ring
                                               of the ornament (fig. 2.3 - 4).

Again, as in the previous project, pay special attention to where you're joining; it is not technically difficult, just make sure the joining is in the right place between the second and the third bead of the beaded picots in the first seven chains of the project.

To work this bracelet from step one:
- Take a double length of Parisian Cotton (about 6 yards for continuous twofold border).
- Needle both tails of the thread (see page 90).
- String **156** beads.
- Load this half of the thread on one shuttle.
- String **100** beads on the other tail and leave it; no knot is necessary with this kind of thread.
- Work seven rings and seven chains of the first row.
- Wind whatever is left of beaded ball thread onto the second shuttle.
- Switch the shuttles for the U-turn chain:

 2 – 2 : 1 ···· 1 : 2 – 2 : 1 ···· 1 : 2 – 2 : 1 ···· 1 : 2 – 2 /~

- Switch the shuttles again to start the second row with a chain: 2 – 2 : 1 + 1 : 2 – 2//.
- Continue the second row joining it by chains to the first row.
- When both rows are joined, complete the pattern with another U-turn chain of three sections:

1) 2 – 2 : 1 ···· 1 : 2 – 2 /~
2) 2 – 2 : 1 ···· 1 : 2 – 2 : 1 ···· 1 : 2 – 2 : 1 ···· 1 : 2 – 2 /~
3) 2 – 2 : 1 +* 1 : 2 – 2//   *the ordinary joining to the beaded picot of section 1)
                                              in this second U-turn chain.

fig. 2.3 - 5

- Attach the second finished U-turn chain to the base of the very first ring
  of the double border (fig. 2.3 - 5).
- Pull the tails on one side.
- Tie square knots and cut the tails.
- Adjust all picots and steam the lacy bracelet into shape.

If you prefer using two shorter thread-lengths instead of a long one, your will have to attach two
loose U-turn chains to the first rings on the opposite ends of the bracelet (fig. 2.3 - 6).

fig. 2.3 - 6

2.4

net of beads

Parisian Cotton thread
3-cut Iris beads #9

The multiple border of this chapter is of the chain-to-ring type.

It makes various netted accessories from purses to screens and wall hangings.

The net is also good for elegant insertions and over-nets in costume design.

The basic pattern adjusts easily to linear and irregular shapes.

key *to the projects:*

R	ring
CH	chain
1, 2, 3...	number of double knots
–	picot
:	1 bead up & 1 bead down
∴	trillium picot of 3 beads
⋯	pointed picot of 3 "up" beads
⋯⋯	flat-top picot of 4 "up" beads
+	ordinary joining
^	final joining
~	switch the shuttles
/	shape & tighten
//	shape, tighten & turn over

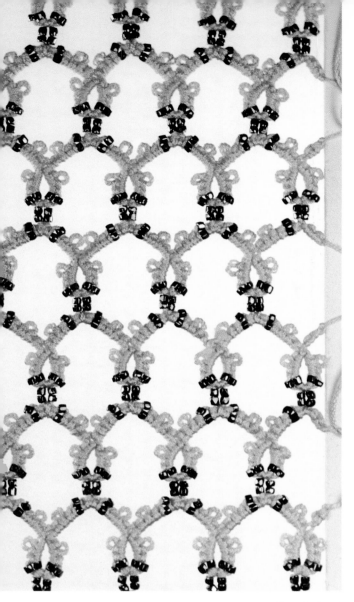

fig. 2.4 - 1

Patterns:

2.4a - *NET for a SCREEN or a WALL-HANGING*

ONE: *R: 2 – 2 : 1 ···· 1 : 2 – 2//
CH: 2 – 2 : 1 ···· 1 : 2 – 2//
  *repeat from here nine more
  times and finish the row with

R: 2 – 2 : 1 ···· 1 : 2 – 2//
CH: 3/
  There are 11 rings and 10
  chains in every odd row.

TWO: *CH: 2 – 2 : 1 + 1 : 2 – 2//
R: 2 – 2 : 1 ···· 1 : 2 – 2//
  *repeat from here nine more
  times and finish the row with

CH: 2 – 2 : 1 + 3 /
  In every even row there are
  only 10 rings and 10 chains.

Keep alternating rows ONE and TWO to make a screen of needed size.

Use the tails at the end of every row to attach the right edge of the screen to the frame.

Since all even rows of the screen are 1 ring shorter than the odd rows there will be gaps along the left edge of the screen. To make up for these gaps along the left edge:
- Take about 15 inches of thread (a good reason to keep sizable pieces of thread).
- Join it to the base of the very first ring in just finished row ONE and make a mini-chain of 3 double stitches.
- Do not cut the tails, they are essential to prepare the screen for framing.
- Work row TWO starting with the ring (see written pattern and the picture above).
- Before starting the next row take another short thread of about 15 inches.
- Join it to the base of the very first ring in row TWO.
- Finish this side with a chain: 2 – 2 : 1 + 3/ joined in a regular way to the flat-top beaded picot of the first ring in the previous row.

The gaps can be filled in either as a finishing touch to the project or at the end of every row.

Reminder: *Before starting any beaded ring, it is necessary to make sure the loop carries the right number of beads.*

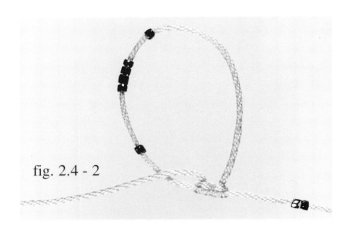

fig. 2.4 - 2

2.4b - *POCKETBOOK / GLASS - CASE*

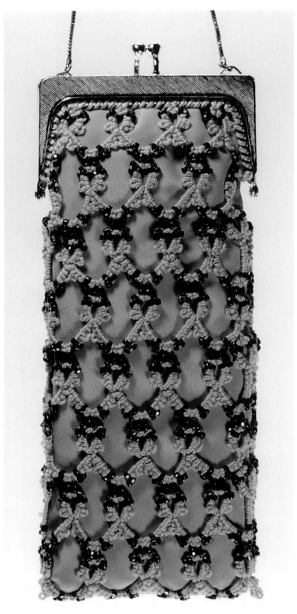

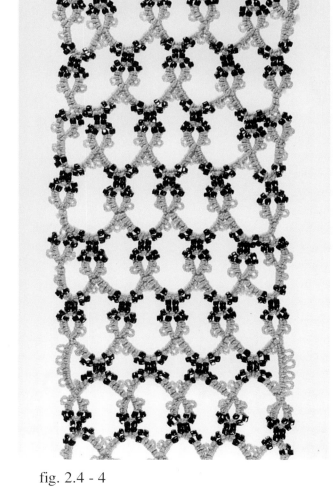

fig. 2.4 - 3   fig. 2.4 - 4

The complete pattern of the pocket book consists of 16 rows: a unit of 2 rows for the bottom part, 10 single rows (5 front + 5 back), and 2 units of 2 rows for back and front top parts. (See the finished pocketbook on fig. 2.4 - 3 and the pattern on fig 2.4 - 4)

Take 2.5 yards of thread and needle it on both tails.
String **116** beads for the shuttle and **48** beads for the ball.
Start the bottom unit working two chain-to-chain stripes as a continuous double border.

  1) *R: 2 – 2 ∴ 1 ···· 1 ∵ 2 – 2//
  2) CH: 2 – 2 ∵ 1 ···· 1∵ 2 – 2//   *repeat from here, until there are 4 rings and
                                            4 chains, it will take you through steps 1 - 8.

  9) R: 2 – 2 ∵ 1 ···· 1 ∵ 2 – 2/~
10) CH: 2 – 2 – 2 – 2 – 2//~
11) R: 2 – 2 ∵ 1 ···· 1 ∵ 2 – 2//
12) CH: 2 – 2 ∵ 1 + 1 ∵ 2 – 2//
13) *R: 2 – 2 ∵ 1 ···· 1 ∵ 2 – 2//   *repeat from here, until there are another
                                            four rings done, and all the chains are connected,
                                            which brings us to step 19:

19) R: 2 – 2 ∵ 1 ···· 1 ∵ 2 – 2/~
20) CH: 2 – 2 – 2 – 2 – 2/^   join to the base of the first ring (fig. 2.4 - 5).

After the bottom of the pocketbook is tatted, the pattern grows in opposite directions as two panels above and under the bottom unit (fig. 2.4 - 4).
Rows 1, 3 and 5 are similar in both panels, row 4 repeats row 2, and rows 6 and 7 make a top unit to fit into glass-case frame.
For one panel without the top unit you will need about 5.5 yards of thread and **394** beads.
Needle the thread on both ends, string 10 - 15 beads on each tail, push them towards the middle of the thread and string the next 10 - 15 beads, then the next.
Please, be careful with thick thread and medium size beads. To protect the thread make some distance between the groups of beads when you slide them along the thread.

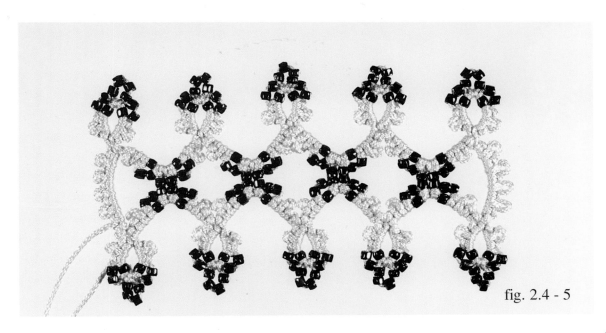

fig. 2.4 - 5

panel row ONE: fig. 2.4 - 6 ↑   ↓ fig. 2.4 - 7   *panel row TWO:*

1) R: 2 – 2 ∵ 1 – 1 ∵ 2 – 2//
2) CH: 3 – 2 ∵ 1 + 1 ∵ 2 – 2//
3) *R: 2 – 2 ∵ 1 ···· 1 ∵ 2 – 2//
4) CH: 2 – 2 ∵ 1 + 1 ∵ 2 – 2//

*repeat steps 3 and 4
two more times*

9) R: 2 – 2 ∵ 1 ···· 1 ∵ 2 – 2//
10) CH: 2 – 2 ∵ 1 + 1 ∵ 2 – 3//
11) R: 2 – 2 ∵ 1 – 1 ∵ 2 – 2/

1) R: 2 – 2 ∵ 1 ···· 1 ∵ 2 – 2//
2) CH: 2 + 2 ∵ 1 + 1 ∵ 2 – 2//
3) R: 2 – 2 ∵ 1 ···· 1 ∵ 2 – 2//
4) CH: 2 – 2 ∵ 1 + 1 ∵ 2 – 2//
5) R: 2 – 2 ∵ 1 ···· 1 ∵ 2 – 2//
6) CH: 2 – 2 ∵ 1 + 1 ∵ 2 – 2//
7) R: 2 – 2 ∵ 1 ···· 1 ∵ 2 – 2//
8) CH: 2 – 2 ∵ 1 + 1 ∵ 2 + 2//
9) R: 2 – 2 ∵ 1 ···· 1 ∵ 2 – 2/

The following pattern of 2 continuous rows has been designed to fit into the pocketbook frame. It can be used either on the opposite ends of the vertical pattern for the glass-case (fig. 2.4 - 3) or at the top of the horizontal pattern for the beaded purse (fig. 2.4 - 9).

1) R: 2 – 2 ∴ 1 ···· 1 ∴ 2 – 2//
2) CH: 2 – 2 ∴ 1 + 1 ∴ 2 – 2//
3) R: 2 – 2 ∴ 1 ···· 1 ∴ 2 – 2//
4) CH: 2 – 2 ∴ 1 + 1 ∴ 2 – 2//
5) R: 2 – 2 ∴ 1 ···· 1 ∴ 2 – 2//
6) CH: 2 – 2 ∴ 1 + 1 ∴ 2 – 2/~
7) CH: 2 – 2 ∴ 1//
8) R: 2 – 2//
9) CH: 1 ∴ 2 – 2//
10) R: 2 – 2 ∴ 1 – 1 ∴ 2 – 2//
11) CH: 2 – 2 ∴ 1 + 1 ∴ 2 – 2//
12) R: 2 – 2 ∴ 1 – 1 ∴ 2 – 2//
13) CH: 2 – 2 ∴ 1 + 1 ∴ 2 – 2//
14) R: 2 – 2 ∴ 1 – 1 ∴ 2 – 2//
15) CH: 2 – 2 ∴ 1 + 1 ∴ 2 – 2//
16) R: 2 – 2 ∴ 1 – 1 ∴ 2 – 2//
17) CH: 2 – 2 ∴ 1 //
18) R: 2 – 2//
19) CH: 1 ∴ 2 – 2 / ~
20) CH: 2 – 2 ∴ 1 + 1 ∴ 2 – 2/^
    join by final joining to the base of the ring in position 1 (fig. 2.4 - 8).

After the bottom unit and five rows in each panel are done, look to the left at the pattern or at the bottom of the page at the picture (fig. 2.4 - 8). It's time for another 2-row continuous pattern, which is a chain-to-ring type, not as symmetrical as the bottom unit pattern, and has to be worked with 2 shuttles.

To work the unit:

- Take about 2.5 yards of Parisian Cotton.
- Fold it in half and mark the center with a very loose over-hand knot.
- Needle both tails of the thread.
- String **58** beads on one tail.
- Wind this half of the thread on shuttle A.
- String **50** beads on the other tail.
- Load this half of the thread on shuttle B.
  Tat the top unit with shuttle A as a shuttle and shuttle B as a ball; start at the lower left ring:
  2 – 2 ∴ 1 ···· 1 ∴ 2 – 2//
Follow the pattern joining chains 2, 4 and 6 to the matching rings in the previous panel row. After the chains 6 and 19 switch the shuttles following the sign (~).
- When chain 20 is done and shaped connect it to the base of ring 1 with the final joining.
- Adjust all the picots, before steaming the piece into shape, and sewing it into the frame.

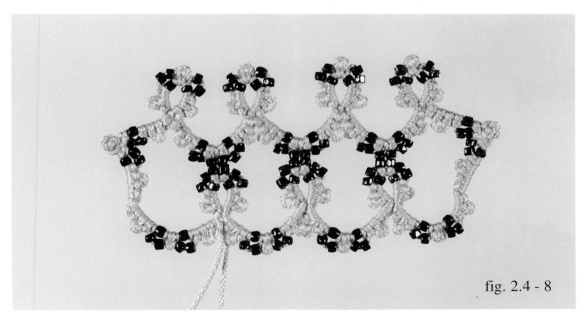

fig. 2.4 - 8

2.4c - BEADED PURSE

2.4c - The pattern for the *BEADED PURSE* (fig. 2.4 - 9) is arranged in five rows. Three long similar rows interconnected chain-to-ring.

The 2-row top units are similar to the top units for the pocketbook pattern, it also has to fit into purse frame (see page 59 and fig. 2.4 - 8).

2.4d - *BEADED BAG* on the opposite page (fig. 2.4 - 10) has a slightly different pattern (fig. 2.4 - 11) since there is no metallic frame here.

This *DRAW-STRING BEADED BAG* is finished with crocheted bottom and with a crocheted edge.

fig. 2.4 - 9

Horizontal pattern of 3 rows for the beaded purse starts at the bottom and grows up:

ONE:
 1) *R: 2 – 2 ∵ 1 – 1 ∵ 2 – 2//
 2) CH: 2 – 2 ∵ 1 – 1 ∵ 2 – 2//   *repeat from here ten more times,

TWO and THREE:
 1) *R: 2 – 2 ∵ 1 – 1 ∵ 2 – 2//
 2) CH: 2 – 2 ∵ 1 + 1 ∵ 2 – 2//   *repeat from here ten more times for each row.

When the three long rows are ready, do top units following the pattern on page 59.
After two top units are attached to the purse body, adjust the picots, steam the project into shape, sew the purse into frame, and tat the long outlining chain divided by final joins into 13 portions:

CH: 2 : 1 : 1 : 1 : 1 ^ 1 : 1 : 1 : 1 : 1 ^ 1 : 1 : 1 : 1 : 1 : 1 : 1 ^ 1 : 1 : 1 ^
    1 : 1 : 1 : 1 : 1 ^ 1 : 1 : 1 : 1 : 1 ^ 1 : 1 : 1 : 1 : 1 ^ 1 : 1 : 1 : 1 : 1 ^
    1 : 1 : 1 ^ 1 : 1 : 1 : 1 : 1 : 1 : 1 : 1 ^ 1 : 1 : 1 : 1 : 1 ^ 1 : 1 : 1 : 1 : 1 ^ 1 : 1 : 1 : 1 : 2 ^

2.4d - *DRAW-STRING BEADED BAG*

fig. 2.4 - 10

1) Work two short separate top pieces:

  *R: 2 – 2 ∵ 1 – 1 ∵ 2 – 2//

  CH: 2 – 2 ∵ 1 ···· 1 ∵ 2 – 2//

     *repeat 3 times, end with the ring.

2) Tat two stripes of 4 rings and 3 chains joined chain-by-chain to those top portions:

  *R: 2 – 2 ∵ 1 ···· 1 ∵ 2 – 2//

  CH: 2 – 2 ∵ 1 + 1 ∵ 2 – 2//

     *repeat 3 times, end with the ring.

3) *R: 2 – 2 ∵ 1 ···· 1 ∵ 2 – 2//

  CH: 2 – 2 ∵ 1 + 1 ∵ 2 – 2//

     *repeat 4 times, joining to one top piece; continue the row with:

  R: 2 – 2 ∵ 1 ···· 1 ∵ 2 – 2//

  CH: 2 – 2 ∵ 1 : 1 : 1 ∵ 2 – 2//

  *R: 2 – 2 ∵ 1 ···· 1 ∵ 2 – 2//

  CH: 2 – 2 ∵ 1 + 1 ∵ 2 – 2//

     *repeat 4 times joining to another top piece, finish the row with:

  R: 2 – 2 ∵ 1 ···· 1 ∵ 2 – 2//

  CH: 2 – 2 ∵ 1 : 1 : 1 ∵ 2 – 2//

For positions 4) and 5) repeat 10 times:

  *R: 2 – 2 ∵ 1 ···· 1 ∵ 2 – 2//

  CH: 2 – 2 ∵ 1 + 1 ∵ 2 – 2//

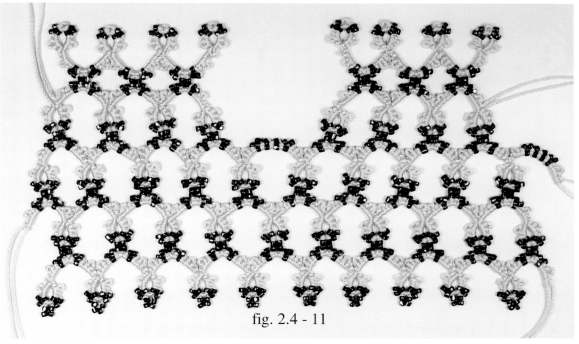

fig. 2.4 - 11

2.4e - *POINTED POCKET TRIMMING*

*The first pattern is a continuous double row, the second pattern is a single row; both worked with 2 shuttles. For the double row you will need **38** beads on one shuttle and **90** beads on another. For the single row string **29** beads on one shuttle and **26** beads on another.*

fig. 2.4 -12

The continuous double row:

1) R: 2 – 2 : 1 ···· 1 : 2 – 2//

2) CH: 2 – 2 : 1 ···· 1 : 2 – 2//

3) R: 2 – 2 : 1 ···· 1 : 2 – 2//

4) CH: 2 – 2 : 1 ···· 1 : 2 – 2//

5) R: 2 – 2 : 1 ···· 1 : 2 – 2//

6) CH: 2 – 2 : 1 ····1 : 2 – 2 : 1····1 : 2 – 2 : 1 : 1 : 2 – 2 : 1····1 : 2 – 2//~

7) CH: 2 – 2 : 1 + 1 : 2 – 2//

8) R: 2 – 2 : 1 ···· 1 : 2 – 2//

9) CH: 2 – 2 : 1 + 1 : 2 – 2//

10) R: 2 – 2 : 1 ···· 1 : 2 – 2//

11) CH: 2 – 2 : 1 + 1 : 2 – 2//~

12) CH: 2 – 2 : 1····1 : 2 – 2 : 1 : 1 : 2 – 2 : 1····1 : 2 – 2 : 1····1 : 2 – 2//^*

*join to the base of the first ring (fig. 2.4 -13).

fig. 2.4 - 13

The single row starts with final joining to the double row at the picot closest to the left (~) mark and ends, also with final joining, at the picot closest to the right (~) mark (see fig. 2.4 - 14).

1) CH: ^1 : 1 : 1 : 2 – 2 : 1 ···· 1 : 2 – 2//~
2) CH: 2 – 2 : 1 + 1 : 2 – 2 : 1 : 1//
3) R: 2 – 3 ∵ 1 ····· 1 ∵ 3 – 2//
4) CH: 1 : 1 : 2 – 2 : 1 + 1 : 2 – 2//~
5) CH: 2 – 2 : 1 ····1 : 2 – 2 : 1 : 1 : 1/^

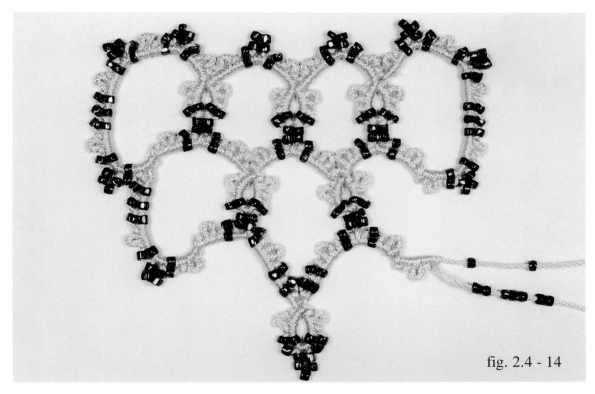

fig. 2.4 - 14

2.5

star motif

Thick cotton thread #3 or #5
3-cut Iris beads #9

The motif can be
a *TREE - DECORATION*.

Two of them make
a *POUCH*.

Wire-framed and
tasseled it becomes
a *DREAM - CATCHER*.

The star/snowflake motifs join
easily and fit well into
repeating patterns for:
BEADED HAIR - NETS,
COSTUME PARTS,
SCREENS,
BOOK-COVERS.

key	*to the projects:*
R	ring
CH	chain
1, 2, 3...	number of double knots
–	picot
:	1 bead up & 1 bead down
∴	trillium picot of 3 beads
·······	long pointed picot of 7 beads
+	regular joining
^	final joining
⊕	swirl joining
/	shape & tighten
//	shape, tighten & turn over

fig. 2.5 - 1

Hexagon, especially *Snow Crystal,* is probably the most popular of all natural motifs.
Designers are fascinated with the shape and use the Snowflake motif extensively.
But as it often happens with familiar things, we do not think much about them, we may even
stop noticing them until something makes us look closely, or differently.
Then this particular look brings a discovery and an avalanche of ideas.

For years a single snowflake has been the most convenient of my special gifts designs.
It is easy, taking less than an hour to string the beads and tat a piece.
The ornament fits well into a greeting card format; it is a joy to give and a pleasure to accept.

The projects in this chapter have been designed while exploring the possibilities of the
Snowflake motif. Another version of the same motif has been designed with an open center for
the dream-catcher. Both designs look spectacular in a variety of repeating patterns.

Reminder: *Before starting any beaded ring, make sure you have on the loop the exact number of beads for this particular ring!*

In this case: **9** "up" beads on the loop, **7** of them for the long pointed picot, plus **2** beads for each side of that picot.
2 "down" beads you'll slide from the shuttle, as needed.

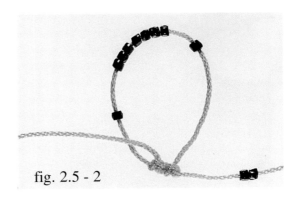

fig. 2.5 - 2

Patterns :

2.5a - SNOWFLAKE

*R: 2 – 2 : 1 ⋯⋯⋯ 1 : 2 – 2//
CH: 4 – 2 : 1 ⋯⋯⋯ 1 : 2 – 4//
　　　　　*repeat from here five
　　　　　　more times to continue
　　　　　　ring-chain pattern.

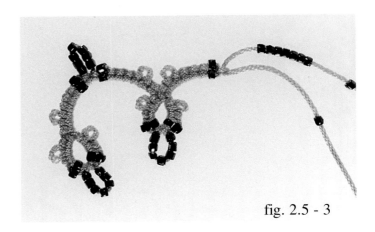

fig. 2.5 - 3

After you have completed the sixth chain, close the center using a needle with beading thread or a piece of fine wire connecting the top beads of long beaded picots (fig. 2.5 - 4).

fig. 2.5 - 4

How to

make a snowflake step by step:

- Take one length (5 - 6 yards) of thread.
- Fold it in half and mark the center with a very loose over-hand knot.
- Needle both tails of the thread (see page 90).

Helpful tip:
To count the needed number of beads look
at figures below: there are 6 rings + 6 chains;
the pattern indicates that on the shuttle thread there are
9 "up" and 2 "down" beads for each of 6 rings +2 "down" beads for every chain of the
ornament, total 78 beads.

- String **78** beads on one tail.
- Load this half of the thread on your shuttle.
- String **54** beads on the second tail: these are "up" beads for the chains.

After you complete the sixth chain:
- Close the center as shown on fig. 2.5 - 4 or fig. 2.5 – 5.
- Join the sixth chain to the base of the first ring.
- Tie a square knot.
- Steam the ornament into shape.
- Use the tails for a string.

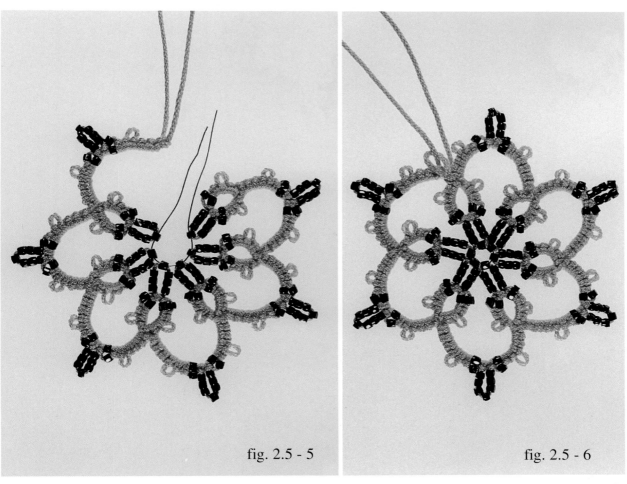

fig. 2.5 - 5

fig. 2.5 - 6

Tracing decorative jeweled containers through history is a subject of special study. I am not trying to squeeze the results of that research into a short paragraph, but cannot resist mentioning a few remarkable facts:
- *We still prefer our protective amulets to look like personal adornments.*
- *Like ancient people we often wear them as necklaces and bracelets, next to our skin, while on the road.*
- *And like many people we still place our amulets on the door-posts.*

Evidently, some things never change, not since we've left Ur for New York.

It seems that tiny beaded bags, lockets, and pouches have their permanent place in our everyday life and art.

The amulet pouches in this chapter have been designed recently. They join a collection started in 1992 with a series of necklace pouches for healing gems.

fig. 2.5 - 7

ONE - the BOTTOM part:

    R: 2 – 2 : 1 ······· 1 : 2 – 2//
    CH: 4 – 2 : 1 ···· 1 : 2 – 4//
        * repeat from here 5 more
          times (see fig. 2.5 - 8).

TWO - the TOP part:

    R: 2 – 2 : 1 ······· 1 : 2 – 2//
    CH: 4 – 2 : 1 + 1 : 2 – 4/
        *repeat from here 5 more times
          (see fig. 2.5 - 9).

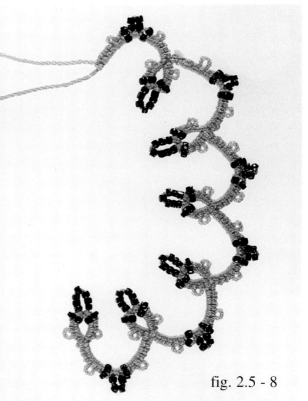

fig. 2.5 - 8

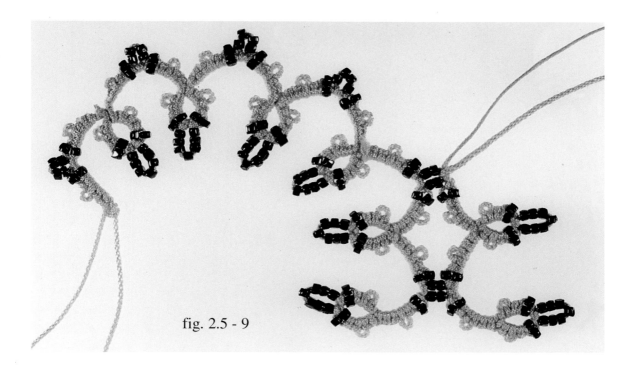

fig. 2.5 - 9

fig. 2.5 - 10

For an *AMULET POUCH* of two similar
motifs (fig. 2.5 - 7):
- Take about 3 yards of Parisian Cotton.
- Needle the tails.
- String **78** beads for the shuttle
  and **36** beads for the ball.
- Work ONE complete motif (pattern **2.5b**).
- Take another length of thread.
- Needle the tails.
- String **78** beads for the shuttle,
  but only **12** for the ball.
- Work the second ornament, joining it to
  the first one as you tat.
- Leave the center open in the second motif.
- Crochet a long string and thread it through
  the long picots of that open center
  to wear the pouch as a necklace.

For a *TASSEL POUCH* (fig. 2.5 - 10):
- Make two connected motifs.
- Leave the centers in both of them open.
- Arrange the string in the upper motif.
- Close the bottom motif with a tassel.
For a tassel you will need 10 - 12 yards of
heavily beaded thread cut in 1-foot pieces.
Thread 2 - 3 of these pieces through each
long picot of the open bottom. Clear the
folded middle parts of the beaded threads and
wrap them tightly. Knot every tail securing
the beads at the needed level.

2.5c - *HANUKAH-GELT BAG #1*

*R : 2 – 2 ∵ 1 ⋯⋯ 1 ∵ 2 – 2//
CH: 4 – 2 ∵ 2 – 2 ∵ 2 – 4//

* from here work 6 repeats total
(see fig. 2.5 -12).

Work two separate motifs (fig. 2.5 - 13).
Finish each motif, that is:
- Close the center.
- Join the last chain to the base of the
  first ring.
- Cut off the tails.
- Adjust picots and steam the pieces
  into shape.
- Put the finished motifs back-to-back
  and join them with a long chain
  either tatted or crocheted.
- Leave an opening for Hanukah money.
- Crochet a string long enough to wear
  the bag as a pouch-necklace.
- Any additional adornments are optional.

fig. 2.5 - 11

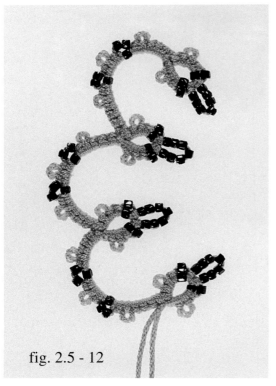

fig. 2.5 - 12

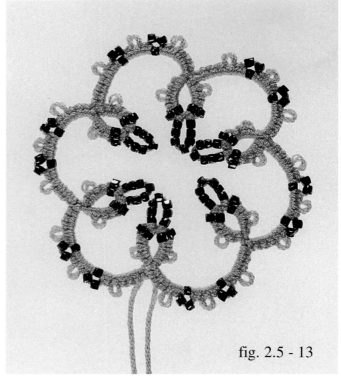

fig. 2.5 - 13

2.5d - *HANUKAH-GELT BAG #2*

To make even simpler version of a bag (fig. 2.5 - 15) work ONE motif:

*R : 2 – 2 : 1 ⋯⋯⋯ 1 : 2 – 2//
CH: 4 – 2 : 2 ⋯⋯ 2 : 2 – 4//
        * from here work 6 repeats total.

After all 6 rings and 6 chains of the first motif are tatted, start the second motif before actually completing the first motif; that is, before closing its center and before joining the last chain to the base of its first ring.
- Work 3 rings alternated by 2 chains.
- When you come to the third chain, start connecting motifs.
- Keep joining the second motif to the first one.
- Chains 1 and 2 should be left unattached in both motifs to make an opening in the bag.
- Chains 3, 4, 5, and 6 will need only **2** "up" beads each (see fig. 2.5 - 14).

After both motifs are connected, complete them joining the sixth chain to the base
of the first ring in both motifs.
Close both centers and add a string long enough to wear the bag as a pouch-necklace.

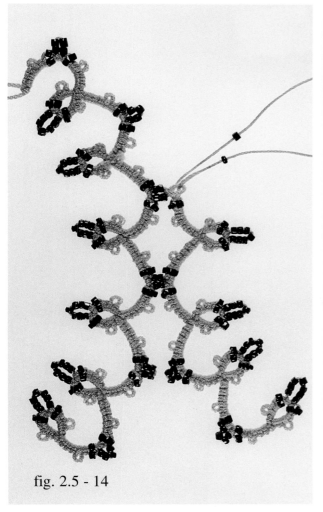

fig. 2.5 - 14

fig. 2.5 - 15

2.5e - DREAM - CATCHER

According to Native American tradition a dream-catcher, being a circle of interlaced strings, has to have an open center to let the good dreams in while the bad ones are caught into that interlaced web.

A dream-catcher has to be a powerful amulet to safeguard a person when he or she is in the most vulnerable stage.

A dream-catcher apparently makes sure that those dreams are enjoyable and that all of them are good.

A dream-catcher may also have additional protective features like a circular frame for a shield and a tassel or a few feathers to scare away evil spirits

fig. 2.5 - 16

fig. 2.5 - 17

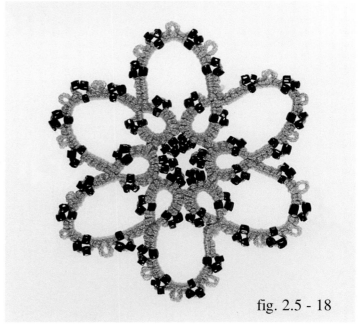

fig. 2.5 - 18

The dream-catcher pattern:

   R: 1 ∵ 3 – 2 ⋯ 2 – 3 ∵ 1//
CH: 4 ∵ 2 – 2 ∵ 2 – 2 ∵ 2 – 2 ∵ 4//
 *R: 1 ∵ 3 + 2 ⋯ 2 – 3 ∵ 1//
CH: 4 ∵ 2 – 2 ∵ 2 – 2 ∵ 2 – 2 ∵ 4//

*repeat from here five times,
finish the main detail for
a dream-catcher (figs. 2.5 - 17, 18).

- Join the sixth chain of the motif to the base of its first ring, tie the tails, and cut them off.
- Steam the motif into shape.
- Take a wire ring or a bangle bracelet with the diameter equal to the width of the motif.
- You can either crochet or wrap that ring, and then stitch the motif onto it.
- Or you may prefer to start crocheting over the ring and attach the motif petals as you crochet.
- When the dream-catcher is framed, it looks like fig. 2.5 - 19.
- Tie the tails and cut them off.
- Crochet a string to wear the amulet as a necklace, or to hang it over a child's bed.
- Make a tassel at the opposite side from the string (fig. 2.5 - 16).

The tassel is an important part, being a protective amulet in its own right.
A few attractive feathers would certainly help to shoo away bad dreams and evil spirits.
Creating an original dream-catcher feel free to add other embellishment (like a string of beads
instead of a crocheted string); it can only make your dream-catcher more effective and powerful.

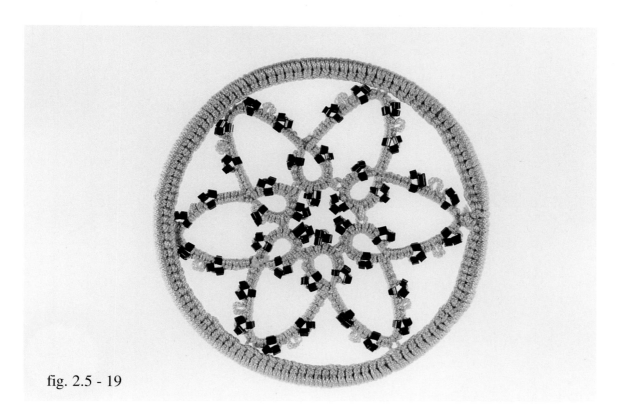

fig. 2.5 - 19

2.5f - *HAT of BEADED NET*

If made in white or silver thread the hat could be a lovely headpiece for a bride.

fig. 2.5 - 20

  R: 1 ∴ 3 − 2 ⋯ 2 − 3 ∴ 1//

CH: 4 ∴ 2 − 2 ∴ 2 − 2 ∴ 2 − 2 ∴ 4//

 *R: 1 ∴ 3 + 2 ⋯ 2 − 3 ∴ 1//

CH: 4 ∴ 2 − 2 ∴ 2 − 2 ∴ 2 − 2 ∴ 4//

      *repeat from here 5 times to make a motif similar to one in fig. 2.5 - 18.

There are seven separate motifs in the pattern for the hat.

To interconnect six exterior motifs and the central one use six smaller units (fig. 2.5 - 21):

R: 1 ∴ 1 − 1 ∴ 1/

R: 1 ∴ 1 − 1 ∴ 1/

R: 1 ∴ 1 − 1 ∴ 1/

To join those six exterior motifs and the rim, use six of the larger three-ring units (fig. 2.5 - 21):

R: 1 ∴ 1 − 1 ∴ 1/

R: 1 ∴ 1 − 1 ∴ 1/

R: 1 ∴ 1 ⋯⋯ 1 ∴ 1/

fig. 2.5 - 21

The rim is a twofold chain-to-chain border very much like the one in chapter **2.3**.

How to
work the hat step-by-step

To make one of the seven similar motifs:
- Take one length (about 3 yards) of thread; fold it in half and mark the center with
  a very loose over-hand knot.
- Needle both tails of the thread (see page 90).

To count the needed number of beads:
Look at the photograph there are 6 rings + 6 chains there.
The pattern indicates that we need on the shuttle thread 7 "up" and 2 "down" beads for each of
those six rings + 4 "down" beads for every chain in the motif, which makes 78 beads.
For each of six small interconnecting units 18 beads are needed.
The larger connecting elements contain 24 beads each.

- String **78** beads on one tail.
- Load this half of the thread on your shuttle.
- String **48** beads on the second tail for those 6 chains.
- Leave this half of the thread as a ball.
- Follow the pattern **2.5f** closely.

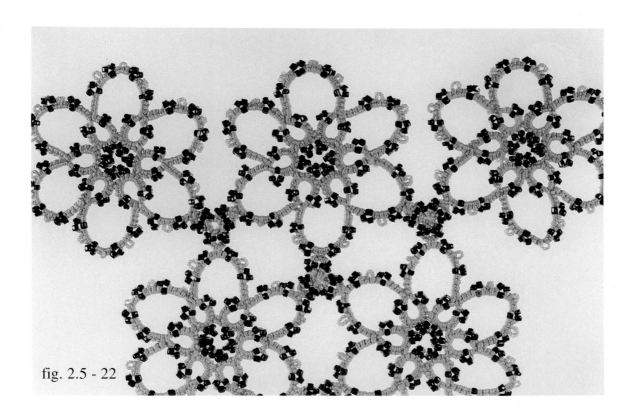

fig. 2.5 - 22

2.5g – *"SNOW COVER" SCREEN*

Helpful: *To count the needed number of beads look at the photograph.*
*There are 6 rings & 6 chains there. The pattern indicates, that we need **9** "up" and **2** "down" beads for each of six rings + **2** "down" beads for every chain of the motif.*
*This amounts to **78** beads on the right shuttle thread.*
*On the left shuttle, which holds your current ball thread, you will need **60** beads:*
***4** for every chain + **6** beads for each of small rings on tops of those chains.*

- Take one length (about 5 yards) of thread; fold it in half and mark the center.
- Needle both tails of the thread.
- String **78** beads on one tail and load this half of the thread on the first shuttle.
- String **24** beads for those 6 chains + **36** beads for the small rings on the outer sides of those chains.
- Load this half of the thread on the second shuttle.

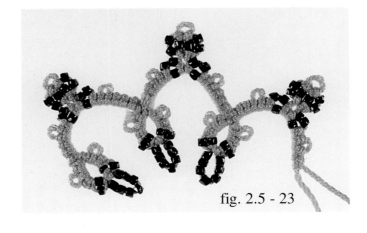

fig. 2.5 - 23

*R: 2 – 2 : 1 ⋯⋯ 1 : 2 – 2//

CH: 4 – 2 ∵ 1/~

  R: 1 ∵ 1 – 1 ∵ 1/~

CH: 1 ∵ 2 – 4//   *repeat from here 5 more times to continue ring-chain pattern.

After you have completed the sixth chain, join it to the base of the first ring and close the center.

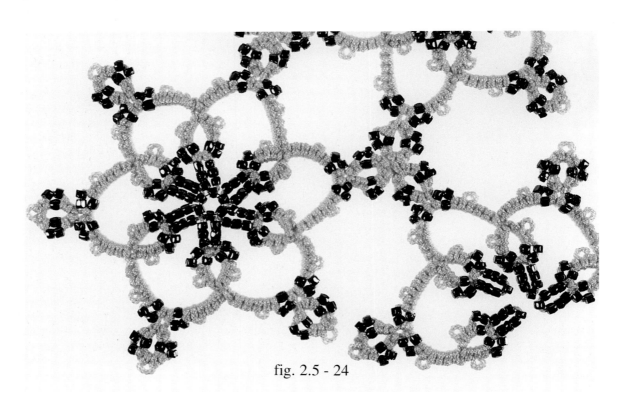

fig. 2.5 - 24

Note: We have been able to tat with one shuttle and a ball using continuous thread, while working five previous projects in this Chapter.
For this particular project we need TWO shuttles loaded with the same continuous thread.

fig. 2.5 - 25

Decorative
Composition
in Beanile Lace

filigree motifs

*As defined in
Webster's New World Dictionary of American English:*

Filigree
*is delicate, lace like ornamental work of
intertwined wire of gold, silver, etc.*

We usually associate the word *filigree* with its first
dictionary meaning of something exceptionally fine,
beautiful, precious, intricately intertwined.
While the word defines primarily an ancient and
powerful combination of thread (*filum*) and seed (*granum*).
In this etymological sense *filigree* stands for every kind
of beadwork from *embroidery* to *weaving*.

Visible or hidden, thread is always there holding and guiding beads.
But to display bead and thread (twined or knotted)
as equally decorative elements we need
LACE of BEADS, a composite ornamental fabric
of two essential elements - *BEAD* and *KNOT*.

Both are mysterious messengers from the depths of history.
Beads and knots are mighty amulets and a favorite personal
adornments in their own right since time immemorial.

As to being mysterious, they certainly are,
even if the greatest mystery is their unceasing popularity.

BEANILE LACE is an original art form
rooted in old traditional crafts of *knotting* and *beading*.

It rediscovers and explores the basic feature of
beads to be threaded, and proves knots
the perfect medium for organizing
thread into lace.

3.1

trefoil

DMC metallic embroidery
thread; HY-MARK glace
thread #12
Fresh-water pearls,
3-cut beads #9

- trefoil -
*an ornamental figure
resembling a threefold leaf,
or a three-leafed plant -
as the clover,
tick trefoil,
and certain species of lotus.* *

----

*Webster's New World Dictionary of
American English

The *trefoil* shape brings together
geometric and plant motifs
closely associated with
beadwork and lace.

Trefoils make
unusual jewelry:
- The opening photo shows
a shoulder pin based on
"rose window" composition.

- Single and double motifs in the
first project have been designed
for pendants or earrings.

Trefoils arranged
in a repeating pattern
turn into
*jeweled accessories
or fabric.*

key *to the projects:*

R	ring
CH	chain
1, 2, 3...	number of double knots
–	picot
:	1 bead up & 1 bead down
∴	trillium picot of 3 beads
⋯	pointed picot of 3 "up" beads
+	ordinary joining
⊕	swirl joining
^	final joining
/	shape & tighten
//	shape, tighten, & turn over

3.1a - *ARRANGING TREFOILS*

fig. 3.1 - 1

String 3-cut amethyst color beads #9 on the
HY-MARK glace thread #12
For one *trefoil* motif you will need **69** beads and
1.5 yards of thread.

1) R: 2∴2 – 2∴2//

2) CH: 2 – 2∴2 – 2 : 1 : 1···1 : 1 : 2 – 2∴2 – 2//

3) R: 2∴2 – 2∴2//

4) CH: 2 – 2∴2 – 2 : 1 : 1···1 : 1 : 2 – 2∴2 – 2//

5) R: 2∴2 ⊕ 2∴2//

6) CH: 2 – 2∴2 – 2 : 1 : 1···1 : 1 : 2 – 2∴2 – 2/^

Be careful: *The thread here is not as friendly and
easy to handle as thick thread of part TWO.
Tatting may seem a little tricky with beads sliding
readily along the thread and getting in your way.*
For the *double trefoil* (fig. 3.1 - 2):
- Tat one motif and put it aside.
- Start a new motif and join it to the previous trefoil
  while working chains 4) and 6).
For the *rose window* composition (fig. 3.1 - 3)
- Join motifs one by one as described above.
- The sixth motif in the composition is connected
  by chains 2), 4), and 6) fitting between the first and
  the fifth motifs.
- To finish the project pull all the tails on one side,
  tie square knots, and cut the tails.

fig. 3.1 - 2

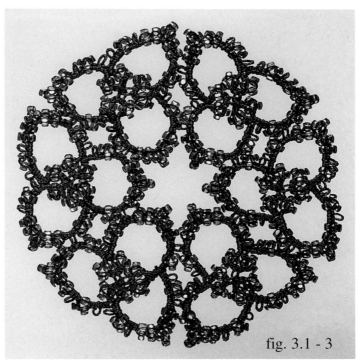

fig. 3.1 - 3

3.1b – *EVENING PURSE*

There are 28 trefoils in this pattern for an evening purse.
Tatted in metallic embroidery thread (DMC light silver thread) and 3-mm garnets, the motifs are interconnected by the picots of their exterior chains to form the shell of the bag.

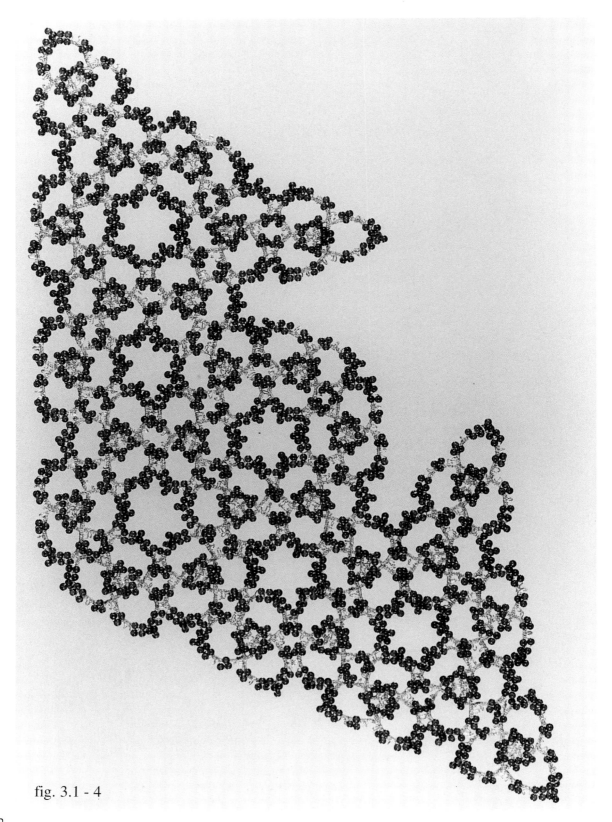

fig. 3.1 - 4

fig. 3.1 - 5

Work 28 trefoil motifs like this:

1) R: 2 ∴ 2 – 2 ∴ 2//

2) CH: 2 – 2 ∴ 2 + 2 : 1 : 1⋯1 : 1 : 2
+ 2 ∴ 2 – 2//

3) R: 2 ∴ 2 – 2 ∴ 2//

4) CH: 2 – 2 ∴ 2 + 2 : 1 : 1⋯1 : 1 : 2
+ 2 ∴ 2 – 2//

5) R: 2 ∴ 2 ⊕ 2 ∴ 2//

6) CH: 2 – 2 ∴ 2 + 2 : 1 : 1⋯1 : 1 : 2
+ 2 ∴ 2 – 2/^

Interconnect them by the chains as you work
the pattern for the evening purse on
the opposite page (fig. 3.1 - 4).

After the shell of the purse is assembled close
the bottom of the purse with a long chain:

1 : 1 : 1 : 1 ∴ 1 : 1 : 1 : 1/^
1 : 1 : 1 – 1 : 1 : 1 – 1 : 1 : 1/^
1 : 1 : 1 – 1 : 1 : 1 – 1 : 1 : 1 – 1 : 1 : 1/^
1 : 1 : 1 – 1 : 1 : 1 – 1 : 1 : 1/^
1 : 1 : 1 – 1 : 1 : 1 – 1 : 1 : 1 – 1 : 1 : 1/^
1 : 1 : 1 – 1 : 1 : 1 – 1 : 1 : 1/^
1 : 1 : 1 – 1 : 1 : 1 – 1 : 1 : 1 – 1 : 1 : 1/^
1 : 1 : 1 – 1 : 1 : 1 – 1 : 1 : 1/^
1 : 1 : 1 : 1 ∴ 1 : 1 : 1 : 1/^

Crochet the ruffle at the top of the purse with
the string threaded through.

3.2

plant scrolls

HY-MARK glace thread #12
3-cut beads #9
TWO shuttles

The beauty and utmost popularity
of *scroll motifs* make any
justification unnecessary.

And it is such a great source of
inspiration and so meaningful,
that to express it adequately
I have to share a few lines from
two wonderful books:

*"Scroll is frequent in nature
as the ram's horn, the nautilus
shell, the vine tendril, etc.
No wonder the motif has been
adapted by many people and
developed subsequently."*

Clarence Pearson Hornung
Handbook of Designs and Devices

*"It is perhaps not without
significance that the generic
Egyptian word for jewelry
appears to refer to imitation
plants and flowers.
…flowers being the first
personal adornments…
and most certainly models and
source of inspiration
for jewelers."*

Cyril Aldred
Jewels of the Pharaohs

key to the projects:

R	ring
CH	chain
1, 2, 3…	number of double knots
–	picot
:	1 bead up & 1 bead down
∴	trillium picot of 3 beads
⋯	pointed picot of 3 "up" beads
⋯⋯	flat-top picot of 4 "up" beads
+	regular joining
∧	final joining
~	switch the shuttles
/	shape & tighten
//	shape, tighten & turn over

Patterns:

3.2 a – LEAF SCROLL

fig. 3.2 - 1

- Needle about 3½ yards of thread on both ends.
- String **142** beads on one tail.
- Wind ¾ of the thread on one shuttle.
- String **23** beads on whatever is left of the opposite tail and wind it on the second shuttle.

Work:

1) R: 2 – 4 : 1 : 1 ⋯ 1 : 1 : 4 – 2/
   Ring of **7** "up" and **4** "down" beads.

2) R: 2 + 4 : 1 : 1 : 1 ⋯ 1 : 1 : 1 : 4 – 2/
   Ring with **10** "up" and **6** "down" beads.

3) R: 2 + 4 : 1 : 1 ⋯ 1 : 1 : 4 – 2//
   Ring of **7** "up" and **4** "down" beads.

4) CH: 1 : 1 : 1 : 1 : 1 : 1 : 1 : 1 : 1 : 1 : 1 : 1/
   Chain of **11** "up" and **11** "down" beads.

5) R: 4 : 1 : 1 ⋯ 1 : 1 : 4//~
   Ring of **7** beads up and **4** beads down:

6) R: 4 : 1 : 1 : 1 ⋯ 1 : 1 : 1 : 4//~
   Ring of **9** beads up and **6** down.

7) Chain of **12** beads up and **12** beads down:
   1 : 1 : 1 : 1 : 1 : 1 : 1 : 1 : 1 : 1 : 1 : 1/

8) R: 2 : 1 : 1 ∴ 1 ⋯ 1 ∴ 1 : 1 : 2//~
   Ring of **11** "up" and **6** "down" beads.

9) R: 2 – 2 : 1 : 1 ⋯ 1 : 1 : 2 – 2/
   Ring of **7** "up" beads and **4** "down" beads.

10) R: 2 – 2 : 1 : 1 ⋯ 1 : 1 : 2 – 2/~
    Ring of **9** "up" beads and **6** "down" beads.

11) Chain of **12** beads up and **12** down beads:
    1 : 1 : 1 : 1 : 1 : 1 : 1 : 1 : 1 : 1 : 1 : 1/ *
    completes the project.

    *Longer chains in a similar project will make it curling.

or the decorative composition at the beginning of part THREE.

The projects **3.2a** & **3.2b** can make a stunning design in Irish Crochet Lace, replacing all or just a few of the crocheted motifs.

If you have a few antique jet-black beads (irregular, uneven, 2-cut or 3-cut, more bugles than seed beads), here is a chance to use them!

However, the pattern may have to be modified, for those beads to fit in.

It is good to re-string old beads, and rearrange them once in a while.

Glass beads, like old pearls, need to be handled and worn to keep glowing.

fig. 3.2 - 2

Pattern:

UPPER RIGHT FLOWER

1) R: 2 ∵ 2 − 2 : 1 : 1 ⋯ 1 : 1 : 2 − 2 ∵ 2/
2) CH: 2 : 1 ∵ 1 ⋯ 1 : 1 ⋯ 1 : 1 ⋯⋯ 1 : 1^
3) CH: 1 ∵ 1 ⋯⋯ 1 : 1 ⋯⋯ 1 ∵ 1/
4) R: 1 ∵ 2 − 2 : 1 : 1 ⋯⋯ 1 : 1 : 2 − 2 ∵ 1/ (on top of chains 2, 3, 5, 6)
5) CH: 1 ∵ 1 ⋯⋯ 1 : 1 ⋯⋯ 1 ∵ 1^ and
6) CH: 1 : 1 ⋯⋯ 1 : 1 ⋯ 1 : 1 ⋯ 1 ∵ 1 : 2^ (to the base of R1)

STEM and LEAVES

7) CH: 1 : 1 : 1 : 1 : 1 : 1 : 1 : 1 : 1 : 1 : 1 : 1//

8) R: 2 – 1 : 1 : 2 – 2 : 1 : 1 ··· 1 : 1 : 2 – 2 : 1 : 1 – 2/~

9) R: 2 ∵ 2 – 2 : 1 : 1 ··· 1 : 1 : 2 – 2 ∵ 2/

10) R: 2 ∵ 1 : 1 : 1 ··· 1 : 1 : 1 ∵ 1/~

11) CH: 1 ∵ 1 : 1 : 1 : 1 : 1 : 1 : 1 : 1 : 1 : 1 : 1/

12) R: 2 ∵ 2 – 2 : 1 : 1 ··· 1 : 1 : 2 – 2 ∵ 2/~

13) R: 2 ∵ 2 – 2 : 1 : 1 ··· 1 : 1 : 2 – 2 ∵ 2//

14) CH: 1 : 1 + 1 : 1 : 1 : 1 : 1 : 1 : 1 : 1 : 1 : 1 : 1//

15) R: 2 ∵ 2 – 2 : 1 : 1 ··· 1 : 1 : 2 – 2 ∵ 2/~

16) R: 2 – 2 ∵ 1 : 1 : 1 ···· 1 : 1 : 1 ∵ 2 – 2/~

17) CH: 1 ∵ 1 : 1 : 1 : 1 : 1 : 1 : 1 : 1 : 1 : 1 : 1–1 : 1 : 1 : 1 : 1 : 1 : 1//

18) R: 1 – 1 : 1 : 1 ∵ 1 + 1 ∵ 1 : 1 : 1 – 1/~

19) R: 1 – 1 : 1 : 1 : 1 ··· 1 : 1 : 1 : 1 – 1/~/

20) CH: 1 ∵ 1 : 1 : 1 : 1 : 1 : 1 : 1 : 1 : 1 : 1 : 1//~

TREFOIL

21) R: 2 ∵ 2 – 2 ∵ 2//

22) CH: 2 – 2 ∵ 2 – 2 : 1 : 1 ··· 1 : 1 : 2 – 2 ∵ 2 – 2//

23) R: 2 ∵ 2 – 2 ∵ 2//

24) CH: 2 – 2 ∵ 2 – 2 : 1 : 1 ··· 1 : 1 : 2 – 2 ∵ 2 – 2//

25) R: 2 ∵ 2 ⊕ 2 ∵ 2//

26) CH: 2 – 2 ∵ 2 – 2 : 1 : 1 ··· 1 : 1 : 2 – 2 ∵ 2 – 2^   (to the base of R 21)

LOWER LEFT FLOWER

27) R: 2 : 1 : 2 – 2 : 1 : 1 ··· 1 : 1 : 2 – 2 : 1 : 2/

28) CH: 2 : 1 : 1 : 1 ··· 1 : 1 ······ 1 : 1^

29) CH: 1 : 1 ······ 1 : 1 ········· 1 : 1 ··········· 1 : 1 ········ 1 : 1 ······ 1 : 1^

30) CH: 1 : 1 ······ 1 : 1 ··· 1 : 1 + (to chain 17) 1 : 1 : 1 : 2^   (to the base of R27)

31) CH: 1 : 1 : 1 : 1 : 1 : 1 : 1 : 1//

32) R: 1 : 1 : 1 ··· 1 : 1 ····· 1 : 1 ··· 1 : 1 : 1//

33) R: 1 : 1 : 1 ··· 1 : 1 ····· 1 : 1 ··· 1 : 1 : 1//

34) CH: 1 : 1 : 1 : 1 : 1 : 1 : 1 : 1 : 1 : 1 : 1 : 1^   (between R18 & R19)

To make the exact copy of the composition in the opening photo of part THREE:
- Follow the pattern **3.2 b** for the plant part. Stitch the ready piece to the background fabric.
- Looking at the opening photo and following the trefoil pattern in Chapter 3.1 try to figure out how to arrange trefoil motifs to fit into the corners of the composition.
- Stretch the fabric with all the details on it and frame the picture.

the techniques

Tatting with beaded thread - - basics, innovations & helpful tips:

This strictly technical part presents essential techniques necessary to acquire and master skills for tatting with beads.

Starting with how to turn thread into needle, string the beads and wind the shuttles.

Including working with beads and tatting simultaneously, making beads fit naturally with tatting stitches.

Some of these methods are original, *invented* especially for tatting with beads.

The others have been *adapted* from a variety of techniques and related needle crafts.

All of them were *improved and refined* during my twelve years of creative tatting and beadwork.

4.1 - *TO NEEDLE the THREAD*

The best way to prepare thread for beading is to use washable, safe, and non-toxic liquid glue.
 Elmer's no run school glue gel is great for this purpose.

- Take a length of thread needed for the project.
For small projects or swatches it's helpful to use a short thread, about 2 yards, and needle both tails.
- Study the thread carefully to see, if it has right or left twist.
- Dip one tail into liquid glue.
- Twist it really tightly following the direction of the thread twist.
- Let it dry, in the meantime work on the other tail.
- You may need to dip the tails into liquid glue again to stiffen the thread.
You will cut these tails off the finished project, so the glue won't ruin the lace.

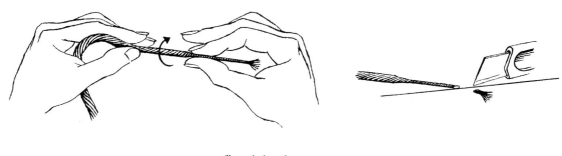

fig. 4.1 - 1

When the thread is needled, put both stiffened tails of the thread on a piece of cardboard, and slash them across the ends with a sharp razor-blade.
String **18 - 20** beads for your first sample onto one tail and leave the second needled tail as it is: do not cut it off, and do not string the beads on. Now you are ready to load the shuttle.

Important!
When it comes to winding beaded thread on the shuttle,
it is helpful to divide beads into groups of 3, 5, or 10 beads, and to leave 5 - 7 inches of thread
without beads between those groups.

The rule of thumb for handling beaded thread is:
- Not to put too many beads on the thread, not to bunch them together, and
- Absolutely not to pull the beads along the thread in a group of considerable numbers.

Always keep in mind that thread is made of fiber, and beads are made of glass, or gems, or metal,
which can cut the thread and ruin a lot of work.
As a rule, thread becomes weaker anyway, with our pushing beads back and forth over it.

A major reason for using short thread and needling it on both ends is to avoid ruining the thread.
You will have to add thread a number of times, especially when you are working on a large project.

PLEASE DO NOT TRY TO SKIP THE ATTACHING PART BY USING LONGER THREAD;
IT IS NOT SAFE, WHEN YOU ARE WORKING WITH BEADS.
IT MAY TURN OUT TIRESOME FOR YOU AND RUINOUS FOR THE THREAD.

4.2 - *HOLDING the THREAD*

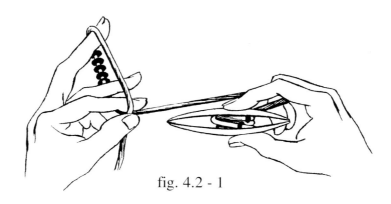

fig. 4.2 - 1

- *Left hand*:

To start a ring
grasp the free end of thread
between thumb and forefinger.
Place the thread **with 5 beads on it***
around the spread fingers crossing it
under the thumb, so that it forms a circle.
The knots are formed
out of this part of the thread.
Extend the middle finger to stretch the
circle and hold it taut, but not too taut.
The middle finger of the left hand
does most of the work
drawing up stitches.

- *Right hand:*

Hold shuttle by flat sides between
thumb and forefinger. Shuttle points to
the left. Thread comes from the back
of the shuttle.

* If you have never tatted, learning how to tat with beads may seem difficult. You might start
  working the patterns at the very beginning of part ONE - *Simply Tatting*.
  These projects are good for initial training. There are no beads there, just double stitches and
  picots. Once you feel at ease with those double stitches and picots, it is not difficult to tat
  with beads. As with any other needlecraft - the more you practice, the easier and more
  enjoyable it becomes.

4.3 - DOUBLE STITCH, *the first half*

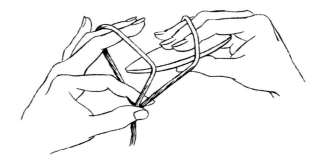

fig. 4.3 - 1

- *Right hand:*

Turn your right hand counter clockwise.
The thread coming from the back of
the shuttle wraps over the fingers of
the right hand.
Without turning the shuttle,
slide it first under, then over the thread
between middle and forefinger
of left hand.

- *Left hand:*

Drop the middle finger,
as soon as the shuttle is out of
that circle.

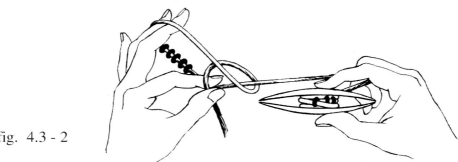

fig. 4.3 - 2

-*Right hand:*

Draw the shuttle thread taut.

The first part of the double stitch is formed out of the thread around left hand:

- *Left hand:*

Extend dropped middle finger,
sliding the stitch down the shuttle thread,
which is held taut. This makes a tight stitch
between thumb and forefinger, completing
the first half of the double stitch.

We can tat an ornamental ring by repeating this part of the double stitch 10-12 times.
This purely decorative ring is called *Josephine picot* in European tradition.
The American term is *Josephine ring*.

4.4 - COMPLETE DOUBLE STITCH and LOOP PICOT

The second part of the double stitch is also formed out of the thread around your left hand.

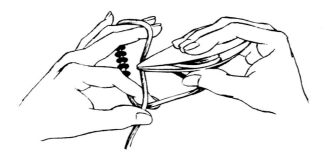

fig. 4.4 - 1

-Right hand:

To tat the second half of a double stitch,
hold the shuttle in horizontal position
and slide it first over, then under
the thread between middle and forefinger
of your left hand.

- Left hand:

Drop the middle finger,
when the shuttle is out of that circle.

-Right hand:

Draw the shuttle thread taut.

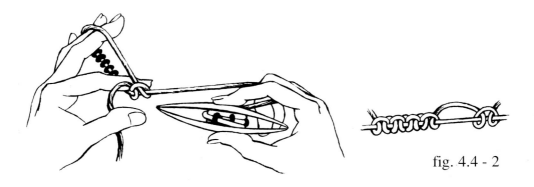

fig. 4.4 - 2

- Left hand:

Extend middle finger to draw up the loop
formed around the shuttle thread as you did
for the first half of the double stitch.

For a sample tat 4 double stitches and start the fifth stitch.
While sliding this first half of the fifth stitch into position pinch it 3 - 5 mm from the preceding
double stitch and tat the second part of the current double stitch.
This makes a *picot* or a *loop picot* - the second of two basic elements in tatting.
Tat 3 double stitches more and pull the shuttle thread to close the ring.
The shuttle thread should move easily inside double stitches of the ring.

The included terms define or explain the specifics of tatting with beads.
It seems convenient to place the list of symbols here, so that you can master the technique hands on, while working the samples, and learning how to read the patterns.

R   means tatted ring.

CH   means tatted chain.

1, 2, 3...   number of double knot stitches in a tatted detail (please do not feel lost, **double knot stitch** has been the original term for this stitch at the turn of the century, meaning that it is a specific stitch, worked as well known double knot. It became **double knot** in European tradition, and **double stitch** to American tatters.

J   Josephine picot or Josephine ring - a decorative ring worked in the first halves of the double stitch.

—   picot or "loop picot" to distinguish it from "bead picot", 4.4 & 4.7.

·   single-bead picot is 1 bead between 2 double stitches, see 4.5.

:   1 "up" bead & 1 "down" bead, that is 1 bead on the left-hand thread balanced by 1 bead from the right-hand thread, see 4.6.

∴   trillium picot formed by 2 beads from the left-hand thread balanced by 1 bead from the right-hand thread, see 4.11.

···   pointed picot consists of 3 "up" beads in a row, see 4.8.

····   4 "up" beads in a row make a flat-top picot, see 4.10.

·······   long beaded picot is of 7 or more "up" beads in a row, 4.9.

+   ordinary joining is the way to connect a current detail to the earlier piece using the left-hand thread; see fig. 4.12 - 2.

^   final joining, known as lock join, connects a chain being tatted currently to a previously tatted ring or chain using the right shuttle thread, see fig. 4.13 - 2 and 4.13 - 3.

⊕   swirl joining connects 3 or 4 tatted details in one point and keeps the bulk out of lacy fabric, see 4.16 and 4.17.

/   shape & tighten: after you have tatted a number of double stitches necessary for a ring or a chain, you have to shape it by pulling the right-hand thread, which moves easily inside tatted stitches and tightens them into snug double knots.

//   shape, tighten & turn over; alternating rings and chains you have to turn a just finished detail upside down: that is, when you start a chain a previously tatted ring should point down; when you start a ring, it is a finished chain that must point down.

———   shuttle A; in diagrams for two-shuttle tatting, you see a solid line marking the path for the first shuttle and dashes marking the second shuttle path.

-------   shuttle B.

~   switch the shuttles means you use one shuttle as a shuttle and another as a ball.

4.5 - RINGS and CHAINS

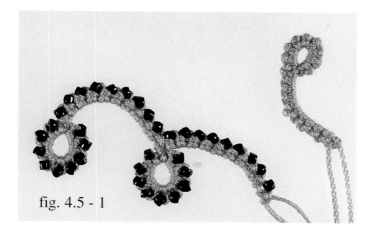

fig. 4.5 - 1

For the chain, you need two sources of thread coming either from two shuttles (see 4.18), or from one shuttle and a ball.
To work a ring/chain sample: load the shuttle (do not cut the thread off the ball); wrap the ball thread over your left-hand fingers. Hold the shuttle horizontally by thumb and forefinger of the right hand, the shuttle points left.

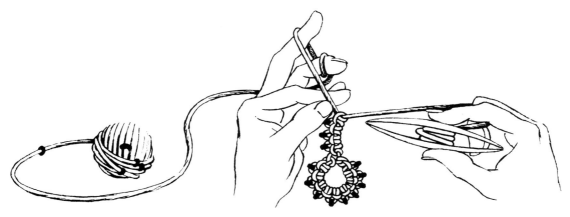

- *Left hand:*

Wind the ball thread over left-hand fingers.
Hold the finished ring between thumb and forefinger of the left hand.

fig. 4.5 - 2

- *Right hand:*

Hold the shuttle pointing left between thumb and forefinger of the right hand.

For a sample (fig. 4.5 - 1, right): tat the ring of 10 double stitches, working the same way you did for the ring, close it, tighten, and turn upside down.
Wrap the thread from the ball over your left hand and tat a chain of 10 double stitches.
To do it with beads (fig. 4.5 - 1, left), you will have to needle both tails of a short (1 yard) thread, string 18 beads on one tail for the shuttle and 18 beads on the other tail for the ball.
Before starting your ring: 1·1·1·1·1·1·1·1·1·1// make sure you have 9 beads on the left-hand circle. Tat 1 double stitch, push 1 bead along the left-hand circle, and tat the next double stitch. Keep going until the ring is done, then tighten it and turn over.
Hold the ring pointing down between thumb and forefinger of the left hand, wrap the ball thread over your left hand, tat 1 double stitch, push one bead from the ball thread, and secure it with the next double stitch. Push another bead from the ball thread and fix it with another double stitch.
After the chain: 1·1·1·1·1·1·1·1·1·1// is done drop the ball (the chain points down and the first ring points up). Tat another ring: 1·1·1·1·1·1·1·1·1·1// using only the shuttle, tighten it, and turn over. Work the second chain: 1·1·1·1·1·1·1·1·1·1//.
In most patterns of alternating rings and chains we use continuous thread and start with a ring.

4.6 - BEADS UP and DOWN

Beanile lace is a portable beadwork of unlimited possibilities in design.

Technically every single "up" bead fills in the space of a picot.

Outlining "up" beads and matching "down" beads turn tatting into ribbon of beads.

The beadwork becomes a kind of tape-lace of beads, as you tat a complete pattern placing beads up and down evenly knotting each pair by one double stitch.

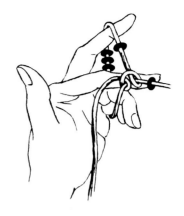

fig. 4.6 - 1

To make a sample (fig. 4.6 - 2, bottom) take 1 yard of a thread #5, needle it on both tails, and string 22 beads #9 for the shuttle and 18 beads for the ball. Before starting the ring: 1·1·1 : 1 : 1 : 1 : 1 : 1 : 1 : 1·1·1// make sure all 11 "up" beads are on your left-hand circle. You will push 7 "down" beads one by one from the shuttle thread as needed.
Tat 1 double stitch, slide 1 "up" bead along the left-hand circle, secure it with a double stitch, repeat once.
Slide the third "up" bead on the left-hand circle and 1 "down" bead from the shuttle. Tat 1 double stitch, repeat 6 times.
Finish the ring fixing each of the last two "up" beads with a double stitch and turn the finished ring upside down. Work the chain: 1 : 1 : 1 : 1 : 1 : 1 : 1 : 1 : 1 : 1 : 1 : 1// with every "up" bead balanced by one bead from the shuttle and fixed with one double stitch.

When we use metallic thread and gem beads, tatting with beads becomes jewelry.
Using round beads of different size changes the shape of beaded rings.

To make the sample of garnets and DMC silver thread #282Z put on the left-hand circle 7 round garnet beads of different size: 1 three-mm bead, 2 four-mm beads, 1 five-mm bead, 2 four-mm beads, and 1 three-mm bead, 7 two-mm "down" beads you will push from the shuttle as needed.

Chain here is a ribbon of 32 two-mm garnets, 16 of which should come from the ball thread, and 16 from the shuttle.

fig. 4.6 - 2

4.7 - PICOT

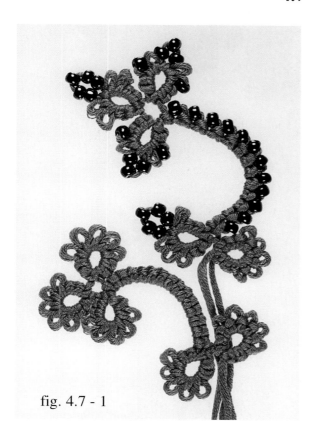

fig. 4.7 - 1

A loop picot can be functional or decorative and sometimes both.

A functional picot provides a joining point and practically marks the place, where rings and chains have to be connected according to a particular pattern.

We use functional picots to attach tatting to fabric, to combine tatting and crochet or tatting and knitting.

Decorative loop picots are often longer to accentuate lacy appearance of tatting.

Beaded picots are the same - functional on occasion, but mostly decorative.

In Beanile lace beads replace loop picots:
- To add color and sparkle to tatting.
- To change the outline of a tatted piece.
- To turn tatting into a complex beadwork of jeweled style.

4.8 - POINTED PICOT

To change the outlining shape of a tatted piece we use pointed or flat-top picots.
If you need a zigzag outline, three beads on the left-hand circle and none on the shuttle thread make it easy and simple. In any case the number of beads depends on the designated length of the picot.

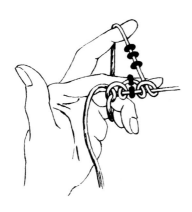

fig. 4.8 - 1

To make a sample of a tiny ring you see started on fig. 4.8 - 1 tat 1 double stitch, slide 1 bead along the left-hand circle and 1 bead from the shuttle.
Tat 1 double stitch.
Move three beads along the left-hand circle and fix them with a double stitch.
Slide the fifth bead along the left-hand circle and balance it with one bead from the shuttle.
Tat 1 double stitch to complete the ring.
Tighten the ring shaping the pointed picot.

Look at fig. 4.7 - 1 and make a sample of the small ring with two single-bead picots, two loop picots and one pointed picot of 3 beads:
R: 2 · 1 – 1 ··· 1 – 1 · 2/.

4.9 - LONG BEADED PICOT

Make a sample ring with long pointed picot

R: 2 – 2 : 1 ⋯⋯⋯ 1 : 2 – 2/

Do not forget that all the "up" beads should be on the left-hand circle before you start the ring.

In this example - 9 "up" beads: 7 for the long, pointed picot and 2 for the smaller bead picots.

To balance those 2 "up" beads you will slide 2 "down" beads from the shuttle as needed.

This ring calls for total of 11 beads.

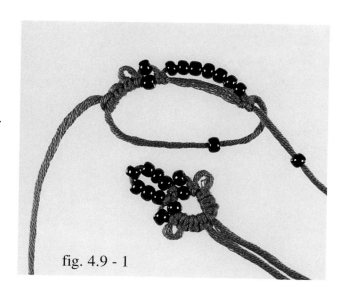

fig. 4.9 - 1

4.10 - FLAT-TOP PICOT

Flat-top picot is a functional beaded picot with even number of beads used to maintain the distance between details in Beanile lace.

In repeating patterns long flat-top picots often become an important part of design.

For a sample work the ring: 2 – 2 : 1 ⋯⋯ 1 : 2 – 2/ having 6 beads on the left-hand circle.

fig. 4.10 - 1

4.11 - TRILLIUM PICOT

To try a *trillium picot* of 3 beads marked (∴) in written patterns tat earrings (fig 4.11 - 1). String 31 beads for one earring, load the shuttle. Before starting the first ring make sure there are 17 beads on your left-hand circle:

R: 1∴1 : 1 : 1 : 1∴1⋯1∴1 : 1 : 1 : 1∴1//.

Turn the finished ring over, start the second ring: 1∴1⋯⋯⋯1∴1/ having 14 beads on your left-hand circle. Close the second ring, tie and cut the tails.

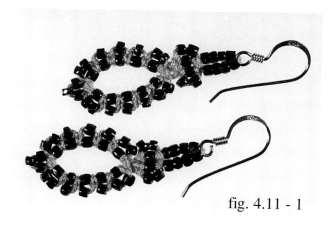

fig. 4.11 - 1

4.12 - *JOINING TATTED ELEMENTS*

You can connect the ring or chain you are currently tatting to an earlier ring or chain.
There are two basic types of joins in tatting:
1 - *The ordinary joining* connects a current detail (ring or chain) to a previously tatted detail using the thread wrapped around the left hand and leaving the right-hand thread free to shape and tighten the current tatted piece when done.
2 - *The final or lock joining* connects a current chain to a previously tatted ring or chain with the shuttle thread. Once the right-hand thread is locked the shape of the chain is fixed.
All shaping must be done before this type of joining (for details on final joining see 4.13).

fig. 4.12 - 1

For a sample of *ordinary joining* (fig. 4.12 - 1) make a ring: $2 - 2 : 1 \cdots 1 : 2 - 2/$ having 5 beads on your left-hand circle before starting it.
Tat the second ring: $2 + 1 : 1 : 1 \cdots\cdots 1 : 1 : 1 - 2/$ as close as possible to the previous ring having 11 beads on the left-hand circle:
- Tat two double stitches.
- Drop the shuttle and pick up a crochet hook.
- Insert the crochet hook through the last picot of the previous ring (fig. 4.12 - 2, left).
- Catch the loop of the current ring (still around your left hand) and draw it up front through the picot far enough for the shuttle to pass.
- Put the crochet hook down, pick up the shuttle and pass it through that loop you've drawn (see fig. 4.12 - 2, center).
- Pull back the circle thread to tighten the connection and complete the second ring.

Start the third ring: $2 - 2 : 1 \cdots 1 : 2 - 2/$ with 5 beads on your left-hand circle (fig. 4.12 - 2, right).
- Make the joining, tighten it and finish the sample.

fig. 4.12 - 2

4.13 - *FINAL or LOCK JOINING*

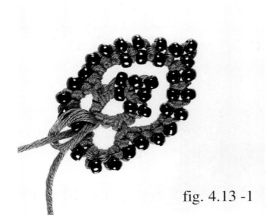

fig. 4.13 -1

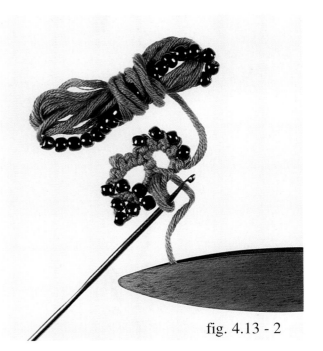

fig. 4.13 - 2

The sample pattern for the ring circled
by a chain with three final joins (fig. 4.13 - 1):

1) R: $2 - 2 : 1 \cdots 1 : 2 - 2$ //
2) CH: $1 \cdot 1 \cdot 1 \cdot 1 \cdot 1 ^\wedge$

   $1 \cdot 1 \cdot 1 \cdot 1 : 1 : 1 : 1 \cdots 1 : 1 : 1 : 1 \cdot 1 \cdot 1 \cdot 1 ^\wedge$

   $1 \cdot 1 \cdot 1 \cdot 1 \cdot 1 ^\wedge$

Work the ring: $2 - 2 : 1 \cdots 1 : 2 - 2$ //, close it, tighten, and turn upside down.

Tat the chain: $1 \cdot 1 \cdot 1 \cdot 1 \cdot 1 /^\wedge$ starting as close to the finished ring as possible; shape it.

Insert the crochet hook into the first plain picot of the ring, and draw the shuttle thread through it.
Pass the shuttle through the loop pointing from the right to the left (fig. 4.13 - 2).
Hold the joining point between thumb and forefinger of your left hand pulling the shuttle
carefully until the join is locked tightly.

Work the central portion of chain: $1 \cdot 1 \cdot 1 \cdot 1 : 1 : 1 : 1 \cdots 1 : 1 : 1 : 1 \cdot 1 \cdot 1 \cdot 1 /^\wedge$
Shape it and make another final joining to the second picot of the ring.

Work the last portion of chain: $1 \cdot 1 \cdot 1 \cdot 1 \cdot 1 /^\wedge$, shape it, and connect to the base of the ring
again using the final joining. Two finished samples like this make a nice pair of earrings.

For a sample of lock-joined chains take two
yards of thread, needle it on both ends and
string 30 beads; 15 for on each tail.
Load two shuttles.
Shuttle A; tat a small ring:
$2 - 2 - 2 - 2 - 2 - 2 - 2 \cdots 2$//.
Work the chain:
$2 - 2 - 2 - 2 - 2 - 2 - 2 \cdots 2$//^~.
Shape it and join with final joining to the last
but one picot on the ring.
Shuttle B; work the chain:
$2 - 2 - 2 - 2 - 2 - 2 - 2 \cdots 2$//^~.
Shape it and join with final joining to the last
but one picot on the previous chain.
Continue the sample, switching the shuttles
after each final joining.

fig. 4.13 - 3

4.14 - *DISTANCED ORNAMENTAL JOINS*

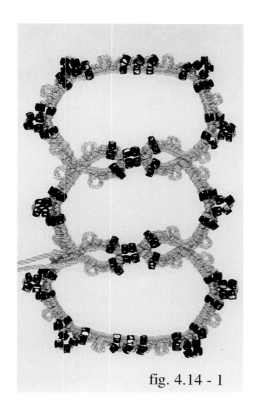

fig. 4.14 - 1

For a sample take about two yards of thread needled on both ends, string 40 beads on one tail.

Wind it on a shuttle, tat the ring: $2 - 2 : 1 \cdots 1 : 2 - 2//$.

String 6 beads on the second tail and work the chain: $2 - 2 : 1 \cdots 1 : 2 - 2//$.

Follow with another ring **R**: $2 - 2 : 1 \cdots 1 : 2 - 2//$.

String 27 beads on the empty tail and work the long chain:
$2 - 2 : 1 \cdots 1 : 2 - 2 : 1 \cdots 1 : 2 - 2 : 1 : 1 : 2 - 2$
$: 1 \cdots 1 : 2 - 2 : 1 \cdots 1 : 2 - 2//$.

Start the next ring: $2 - 2 : 1 + 1 : 2 - 2$, which has to be joined to the center of the last ring.

Now there are only two beads on your left-hand circle.

Work $2 - 2 : 1$ and join the current ring to the long picot of the last finished ring, inserting the crochet hook between the second and the third beads.

Complete the current ring: $1 : 2 - 2//$.

Finish the sample looking at the picture on the left.
When tatted pieces are joined and tightened, there are beads arranged into I-shape between them.

This joining makes a distance between tatted pieces equal to a half number of beads used for a long flat-top picot.

4.15 - *DIAMOND SHAPE ORNAMENTAL JOINING*

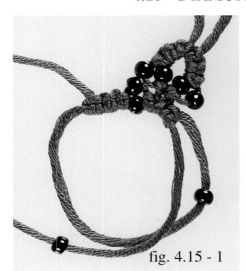

fig. 4.15 - 1

fig. 4.15 - 2

Work the ring: $2 - 2 : 1 - 1 : 2 - 2/$.

That is, tat 2 double stitches, picot, 2 double stitches, then place 1 bead up and 1 bead down and secure them with the fifth double knot stitch.

Make central picot; close it with the sixth double stitch. Place 1 bead up and 1 bead down; secure them with the seventh and the eighth double stitches. Work another plain picot, finish the ring with two double stitches, close it.

Start the similar beaded ring following the same pattern: Work $2 - 2 : 1$ (fig. 4.15 - 1), join to the central picot of the first ring, complete the current ring: with: $1 : 2 - 2//$.

When both rings are joined and tightened, there are 8 beads arranged into diamond shape between them (fig. 4.15 - 2).

There is a special ornamental effect, when you use *trillium picots* as side picots for the connection point.
See section 4.17 for details.

101

4.16 - *SWIRLS and LOCKS #1*

Here is another innovative joining, which can be very useful for both bead tatting (see projects in chapter 3.1) and general tatting (see chapters 1.5, 1.6, and 1.10).
It keeps the "bulk" out of lacy fabric when three or four rings are joined in a single point.
Swirl makes it easier, replacing multiple joins and providing a clear, neat connecting point.

As a sample try this pattern of 4 alternating rings and chains connected in central point.
Work positions 1 – 6. Starting ring 7, tat:
2 – 1 : 1 : 1, insert crochet hook into central picots of the rings 1, 3, 5.

Draw out the loop of the left-hand circle thread large enough for the shuttle to pass and make an ordinary joining.
Finish the current ring: 1 : 1 : 1 – 2//.
Work chain 8 and lock-join it to the base of ring 1 (see 4.12 and 4.13 about joins).

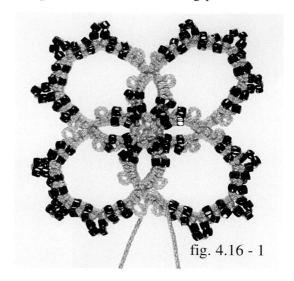

fig. 4.16 - 1

1) R: 2 – 1 : 1 : 1 – 1 : 1 : 1 – 2//
2) CH: 2 – 1 : 1 : 1 ···· 1 :1 :1 ···· 1 :1 :1 ···· 1 :1 : 1 – 2//
3) R: 2 – 1 : 1 : 1 – 1 : 1 : 1 – 2//
4) CH: 2 – 1 : 1 : 1····1 : 1 : 1····1 : 1 : 1 ···· 1 : 1 : 1 – 2//
5) R: 2 – 1 : 1 : 1 – 1 : 1 : 1 – 2//
6) CH: 2 – 1 : 1 : 1 ···· 1 : 1 : 1 ···· 1 : 1 : 1 ···· 1 : 1 : 1 – 2//
7) R: 2 – 1 : 1 : 1 ⊕ 1 : 1 : 1 – 2//
8) CH: 2 – 1 : 1 : 1 ···· 1 : 1 : 1 ···· 1 : 1 : 1 ···· 1 : 1 : 1 – 2//^

4.17 – *SWIRLS and LOCKS #2*

Pattern of the *trefoil motif* with swirl joining:
1) R: 2 ∴ 2 – 2 ∴ 2//
2) CH: 2– 2∴2 – 2 : 1 : 1···1 : 1 : 2 – 2∴2– 2//
3) R: 2 ∴ 2 – 2 ∴ 2//
4) CH: 2– 2∴2 – 2 : 1 : 1···1 : 1 : 2 – 2∴2– 2//
5) R: 2 ∴ 2 ⊕ 2 ∴ 2//
6) CH: 2– 2∴2– 2 : 1 : 1···1 : 1 : 2– 2∴2– 2//^

fig. 4.17 - 1

4.18 - *CONTINUOUS PATTERNS*

I believe the continuous "one - two - three rows" patterns have great possibilities in designing tatted lace. The possibilities are greater if you tat with two shuttles, and they are limitless when you tat with beads. To work with two shuttles take 2 - 3 yards of thread, fold it in half, and mark the middle with a very loose overhand knot. Wind one half of this thread on one shuttle, and the other half on the second shuttle. This gives you a continuous thread to tat with.

fig. 4.18 - 1

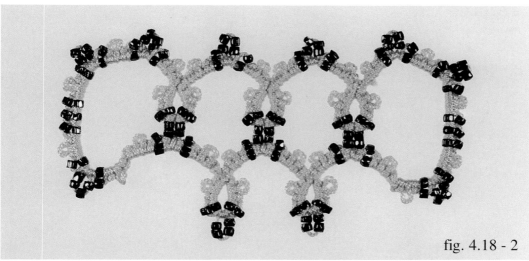

fig. 4.18 - 2

No extra tails, no turning back;
One consecutive sinuous path of ups and downs
Which neatly brings us back to the starting point down the road.

At the beginning of a journey we move forward lingering at places
Or wandering around for a while.
May even fall into adventure, only to enjoy every minute of climbing out.

When everything is done and tatted,
With the very last of carefully counted beads and stitches in place,
Here we are, coming home safely.

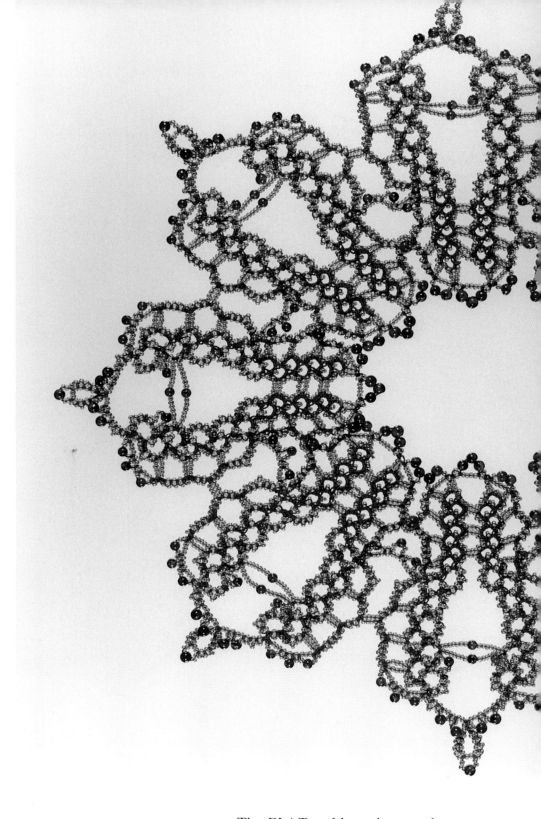

farewell

The *ELAT* necklace above and
the *GOLDEN LOTUS* shoulder pendant
on the opposite page
are parts of the Beanile collection
inspired by the breath-taking view of the
Red Sea and Sinai.

Both pieces will be presented in a future
publication on Beanile lace.

to commuters,

travelers and others

of nomadic tribes :

It's helpful,
Whenever you have time and place,
To needle a bunch of different threads,
And pre-string the beads
For various projects.

    It's always convenient and
    Always a great joy
    (be it inside 747 crossing Atlantic or
    on a horse-back in the middle of nowhere)
    To take the sparkling ball
    Out of your pocket / saddle-bag,
    And start working.

With the beads safely threaded,
Not rolling off,
And not trying to become lost.
Nothing breaks the beauty of the moment,
The spell-casting rhythm of hands dancing,
When beads fit into place, each flanked by a knot.

    The shuttle keeps flying.
    The design unfolds graciously.

glossary

Amulet pouch: a small often lavishly ornamented bag or a tiny jeweled container worn as a necklace for good luck and protection.

Ball thread (working thread): thread wrapped around the left hand; out of this thread all the double stitches are formed.

Beaded lace: lace worked in a thread with beads on it.

Bead down: a bead coming into tatting from the right-hand thread.

Bead up: a bead placed on the left-hand circle for the ring, or on the ball thread for the chain.

Beanile lace: is a composite of *beads* and *knots* with beads first threaded, then tatted into lace.

Border: a narrow stripe, often ornamental, along an edge.

Bugles: tube-shaped glass beads.

Beadwork: art created with small, uniform beads (generally seed beads), in which the beads are subordinate to the overall form and design of the entire piece.

Chain (single chain): an element in tatting, worked with two sources of thread.

Chain-to-chain: the way to connect details in tatted lace.

Chain-to-ring: connecting a currently worked chain to an earlier tatted ring.

Continuous thread: thread connecting two loaded shuttles or a shuttle and a ball.

Crochet: fabric built up of chain stitches worked with a crochet hook.

Cut-work: an embroidered lace formed by the removal of shapes of woven fabric.

Double border or twofold border: two narrow stripes connected by similar edges.

Double knot stitch: at the turn of the century the original term for the stitch in tatting, worked as well known double knot. Later it became *double knot* in European tradition, and *double stitch* to American tatters.

Distanced ornamental joining: connects elements and details at a distance measured by the number of beads on the long flat-top picot.

Edge: usually an outer edge, which is either scalloped or ornamented with picots.

Edging: narrow lace designed to be attached by one edge only.

Fillet: a narrow band.

Final or lock joining: type of joining where the same right-hand thread forms a loop and an end passing through the loop to make a connecting knot.

Finger tatting: tatting with no tools, just fingers.

Flat-top picot: in Beanile lace a long picot formed by even number of beads.

Flounce: wide, ornamental ruffle.

Hanukah-gelt bag: in Yiddish tradition, a small bag with some money makes a Hanukkah gift for children.

Insertion: stripe of lace, usually with two straight edges, to be sewed between two pieces of fabric, also a medallion sewed into a cutout area.

Iris or iridescent beads: multicolored glass beads with rainbow-like play of colors.

Joined chains: chains connected to each other in tatted lace design, as an opposite to single unattached chains.

Josephine picot or Josephine ring: decorative ring worked in first halves of double stitch.

Key for the project: list of symbols necessary to follow the pattern while working a project.

Knot: a lump or knob in a thread formed by passing one end, free or wound on a shuttle, through a loop and drawing it tight.

Loop picot: in tatting and bead tatting - part of a plain thread between two double stitches.

Meandering chains: chains worked with different shuttles and pointing in opposite directions.

Motif: an individual design element, or a portion, often recurring, of a larger pattern, such as a flower, a leaf, or a geometric figure.

Multiple border: numerous narrow stripes connected by their edges and forming a kind of beaded net, or very open beaded fabric.

Needle the thread: prepare the hardened tail of a thread by twisting glue into it.

Open work: word applied indifferently to embroidery, lace-making, knitting, netting, cut-work, and crochet, and signifying the interstices between the several portions of close work.

Ordinary joining: in tatting - regular joining with the left-hand thread.

Ornament: anything serving to adorn; decoration, embellishment.

Outlining rings: rings on the outer edge of a curve or a motif.

Picots: little loops along the outline of a lace; functional or decorating parts of the design.

Pointed picot: in Beanile lace a picot of 3, 5, or 7 beads on the left-hand thread with no beads on the shuttle thread.

Ribbon effect: special effect in bead tatting. The beads are placed on both working threads evenly – one up, one down with a double stitch dividing each pair.
The technique turns tatting into beadwork.

Ring-chain module: of one ring and one chain alternating in a design to form a pattern.

Seed beads: small round beads, glass.

Shuttle tatting: working double stitches with thread wound on a shuttle, as opposed to needle tatting or finger tatting.

Shuttle thread: in tatting, thread coming from the right-hand shuttle.

Stripe: a narrow band.

Square knot: a double knot, in which the free ends run parallel to the standing part.

Switch the shuttles: alternate positions of shuttles in two-shuttle tatting.

Swirl joining: swirl joining connects 3 or 4 tatted details in one point and keeps the bulk out of lacy fabric.

Three-cut beads: beads having faceted sides and ends.

Trillium picot: in Beanile lace a picot formed by two beads on the left-hand thread and one bead from the shuttle or the right-hand thread.

Two-cut beads: beads having faceted sides.

select bibliography

Beadwork

Banes, Helen, and Fitzgerald, Diane. *Beads and Threads: A New Technique for Fiber Jewelry.* Simon & Schuster, 1994.

Campbell-Harding, Valerie, and Watts,Pamela. *Bead Embroidery.* Lacis Publications, 1993.

Coles, Janet, and Budwig, Robert. *The Book of Beads: A Practical and Inspirational Guide to Beads and Jewelry Making.* Simon & Schuster, 1990.

Coles , Janet. *Beads: An Exploration of Bead Traditions Around the World.* Simon & Schuster, 1997.

Creative Bead Jewelry: Weaving, Looming, Stringing, Wiring. Lark Books, 1995.

Dubin , Lois Sherr. *The History of Beads: From 30,000 BC to the Present.* Harry N. Abrams, 1995.

Hickman, Julia. *Decorative Needlepoint: Tapestry and Beadwork.* Reader's Digest, 1993.

Ragan, Genie. *Beads: The Art of Stringing.* Gem Guides Book Co., 1986.

Sterbenz, Carol Endler, and Gross Gay Merill. *Buttons, Beads, Ribbons, and Lace.* (Simply Sensational Series), Crescent Books, 1994.

Tatting

Auld, Rhoda L. *Tatting: the contemporary Art of Knotting With a Shuttle.* Simon & Schuster, 1984.

Clark's Book # 183. The Spool Cotton Company, 1942.

Clark's Book # 207. The Spool Cotton Company, 1944.

Hoare, Katharin L. *The Art of Tatting.* Lacis Publications, 1982.

Morgan, Lael. *Tatting: A New Look at the Old Art of Making Lace.* Doubleday, 1977.

Nichols, Elgiva. *Tatting: Technique and History,* Dover Publications, Inc., 1984.

Nichols, Elgiva. A. *Tatting Techniques: Old Revivals and New Experiments,* Scribner, 1976.

Orr, Anne. *Ann Orr's Classic Tatting Patterns.* Dover Publications, Inc., 1985.

Orr, Anne. *Tatting with Anne Orr.* Am. Thread 1935. Reprint by Dover Publications, Inc., New York, 1989.

Waldrep, Mary C. *The Tatter's Treasure Chest.* (Dover Needlework Series), Dover Publications, Inc., 1992.

Waller, Irene. *Tatting: A Contemporary Art Form.* NTC / Contemporary Publishing, 1974.

Helpful

Boyd, Margaret A. *The Crafts Supply Source Book.* Betterway Books, Cincinnati, Ohio, 1996.
    A comprehensive shop-by-mail guide for thousands of craft materials.

The following short list includes the books which became essential reference sources in my years of researching beads, knots, and their place in the phenomenon of ornament.

Aldred, Cyril. *Jewels of the Pharaohs*. Thames and Hudson Ltd, London, 1971.
This book presents nearly 200 objects from collections all over the world. The author explains the fascinating uses and significance of Egyptian jewels, the materials, and the techniques, paying special attention to the techniques of stringing beads and to the craft of arranging beads into collar-necklaces.
The text is illustrated throughout with line drawings in addition to photographs.
One of the most distinguished Egyptologists of our time, Cyril Aldred, traces the origins of beads and jewelry to the ornamental forms derived from nature, which stay popular for centuries in different cultures.

Edwards, Joan. *Bead Embroidery*. LACIS, Berkeley, California, 1992.
The author explores in detail most of the techniques for incorporating beads into textiles, mentioning each known way of arranging beads on a thread, which makes it a great reference book. The instructions given for a variety of techniques make it a practical book and a source of inspiration for bead lovers.

Faleeva, Valeria A. *Russian Pillow Lace* (Russian). Khudoznik RSFSR, Leningrad, 1983.
The book by one of the greatest experts in Russian textiles is the result of research on pillow lace in different regions of Russia, featuring every type of lace with their characteristic patterns and details of design

Faleeva, Valeria A., and Moiseenko, Elena. *Bead & Bugle Embroidery in Russia*. Khudoznik RSFSR, Leningrad, 1990.
The two distinguished experts in Russian textiles trace and guide you through the rich history and remarkable popularity of beads and diversity of beadwork in Russia in the $18^{th} - 20^{th}$ centuries.
The book is based on the most important collections of beadwork from the Historical Museum, Moscow and from the Hermitage, the Russian Museum, and the Museum of Ethnography, Leningrad (St. Petersburg).

Haering, Evelyn. *Antique Combs & Purses*. Gallery Graphics Press, Carmel, California, 1983.
This is the first book which covers the origin and development of combs and purses. It is of great help to anyone who wishes to learn more about types, origins and production of these useful and decorative items. The book includes numerous references and lists important sources of supplies and information.

Hornung, Clarence Pearson. *Handbook of Designs and Devices*. Dover Publications, NY, 1946.
This book first published in 1932 includes 1836 geometric elements drawn by the author as a result of a close study of the arts of design in ancient Egypt, Greece, Arabia, and Japan, where the geometric and abstract design have been dominant. Mr. Hornung, a practical designer and a student of decorative forms, explores a general foundation for decorative design - the geometry of space division. The author manages to compile a decorative alphabet of abstract and simple forms applicable to different types of design and open to almost infinite variation.

Jackson, F. Nevill, Mrs. *Old Handmade Lace with a Dictionary of Lace*. Dover Publications, Inc., NY, 1987.
This rare and attractive turn-of-the-century history of lace guides textile and history lovers through centuries of lace-making magic.

Leeming, Joseph. *Fun with String*. Dover Publications, Inc, NY, 1974. Republication of the work originally published in 1940 by J. B. Lippincott Company.
This small book is a collection of string games, useful braiding and weaving, knot work, and magic with string and rope.

Palliser, Bury, Mrs. *History of Lace*. Republication of the 4th edition 1911. Dover Publications, Inc., New York, 1984.
The book touches on the ancient history of textiles and covers the history and development of European lace-making through $17^{th} - 19^{th}$ centuries.

Schumann, Walter. *Gemstones of the World*. Sterling Publishing Co., Inc., New York, 1977.
This comprehensive and compact reference book gives classification of stones, their names and characteristics, their symbolic meanings, and healing properties.

Shaw, George Russell. *Knots, Useful and Ornamental*. 3rd ed., New York, Macmillan, 1972.

Warnick, Kathleen, and Nilsson Shirley. *Legacy of Lace,* Crown Publishers, Inc., New York, 1988.
A book on identifying, collecting, and preserving lace.

Wilson, Eva. *Ornament 8,000 Years an Illustrated Handbook of Motifs*. Harry N. Abrams, Inc., Publishers, 1994.
The book features a vast variety of ornamental motifs: from spirals, scrolls, and meanders to rosette, intersecting circles, and geometrical constructions, tracing them all over the world and 8,000 years back.

publisher's notes on materials

"Parisian" Cotton: A (4) 2-ply twisted cotton thread having a chainette appearance of a thickness similar to #10 crochet cotton. Made in France. Put up on 20 yd tubes. (RB01)

"Cebelia" Cotton: A DMC 3-ply cotton thread. Sizes used for projects are #5 and #10.

Metallic Embroidery Thread: DMC Metallic thread available in 43.7 yard spools. Available in Antique Gold (273Z), Antique Silver (274Z), Gold (s84Z), Light Gold (282Z), Light Silver (285Z), and Multi Color (275Z)

"HY-MARK" Glace Thread: Available in size #12, similar in thickness to #30 crochet cotton. This is an extremely strong 4-ply twisted cotton thread with a coating of polyester giving it a polished finish. Available on 400 yd spools in black and white.

Purse Frames used in projects are manufactured by LACIS and are available in sterling silver plate or gold plate finish. Frames illustrated: Page 56 - LS81; Page 60 – LS73.

Crochet Hooks: Used for joinings, sizes #6 or #7 suggested.

Beads: #9 3-cut seed beads.

Gemstone Beads: 3mm Garnet

Pearls: Fresh water irregular shape beads, 3-4 mm

Black Beads: #11 seed beads, matte or bright finish

The above materials should be available from the suppliers listed on page 111. For further information contact this publisher

resources

Limited tatting supplies and beads can be found at most craft stores. The following shops are noted for their extensive line of beads, shuttles, specialty threads and other tatting supplies.

LACIS
2982 Adeline Street
Berkeley CA 94703

HANDY HANDS
RR1, Box 4
Paxton IL 60957

SNOWGOOSE
1880 S. Pierce #4
Lakewood CO 80232

BEGGARS' LACE
182 S. Reed St
Lakewood CO 80226

INGEBRETSEN'S
1601 E. Lake St.
Minneapolis MN 55407

LACEWORK
411 S.E. 5th St.
Bartlesville OK 74003

UNICORN BOOKS AND CRAFTS
1338 Ross St.
Petaluma CA 94954

VELONA NEEDLEWORKS
5753 D. Santa Ana Canyon Rd.
Anaheim CA 92807

YARN BARN
930 Massachusetts
Lawrence KS 66044

YARN BARN OF SAN ANTONIO
4300 McCullough
San Antonio TX 78212

HELBY IMPORT
1501 S. Park Ave.
Linden NJ 07036

FIRE MOUNTAIN GEMS
28195 Redwood Hwy
Cave Junction OR 97523

sources for information

INTERNATIONAL OLD LACERS
% Julie Hendrick
2737 NE 98th
Seattle WA 98115

BEAD AND BUTTON (Magazine)
Kalmbach Publishing Co.
21027 Crossroads Circle
PO Box 1612
Waukesha WI 53187-1612

INTERWEAVE BEADWORK
Interweave Press, Inc.
201 East Fourth Street
Loveland CO 80537-5655

LAPIDARY JOURNAL
PO Box 302
Devon PA 19333-9903

LACIS publishes and distributes books specifically related to the textile arts, focusing on the subjects of lace and lace making, tatting, costume, embroidery and hand sewing.

Other LACIS books on tatting:

TATTING: DESIGNS FROM VICTORIAN LACE CRAFT, ed.by Jules & Kaethe Kliot
BEADS IN TATTING, Judith Connors
THE COMPLETE BOOK OF TATTING, Rebecca Jones
THE ART OF TATTING, Katherine Hoare
TATTING WITH VISUAL PATTERNS, Mary Konior
PRACTICAL TATTING, Phyllis Sparks
NEW DIMENSIONS IN TATTING, To de Haan-van Beek

Other LACIS books of interest:

THE CARE AND PRESERVATION OF TEXTILES, Karen Finch & Greta Putnam
THE ART OF HAIR WORK, Mark Campbell
THE ART AND CRAFT OF RIBBON WORK, ed by Jules & Kaethe Kliot
SMOCKING AND GATHERING FOR FABRIC MANIPULATION, Nellie Weymouth Link
DRAFTING AND PATTERN DESIGNING (1926), Women's Institute of Domestic Arts
GARMENT PATTERNS, 1889, ed by Jules & Kaethe Kliot
MILLINERY FOR EVERY WOMAN, Georgina Kerr Kaye
THE TECHNIQUE OF LADIES' HAIR DRESSING (19th c.): Mark Campbell & A. Mallemont
HAUTE COUTURE EMBROIDERY: THE ART OF LESAGE, Palmer White
THE MARY FRANCES SEWING BOOK, Jane Eayre Fryer
THE MARY FRANCES KNITTING AND CROCHETING BOOK, Jane Eayre Fryer
THE MARY FRANCES HOUSEKEEPER, Jane Eayre Fryer
THE MARY FRANCES COOK BOOK, Jane Eayre Fryer
BATTENBERG AND POINT LACE, Nellie Clarke Brown
BATTENBERG LACE PATTERN BOOK, ed. Jules & Kaethe Kliot
NEEDLE LACES, BATTENBERG POINT & RETICELLA, ed. Jules & Kaethe Kliot
CROCHET: EDGINGS & INSERTIONS, Eliza A. Taylor & Belle Robinson
CROCHET: EDGINGS & MORE, ed. Jules & Kaethe Kliot
CROCHET: NOVELTIES, ed. Jules & Kaethe Kliot
CROCHET: MORE EDGINGS, ed. Jules & Kaethe Kliot
MACRAMÉ, SOURCES OF FINE KNOTTING, ed Jules & Kaethe Kliot
THE NEEDLE MADE LACES OF RETICELLA, ed Jules & Kaethe Kliot
CASALGUIDI STYLE LINEN EMBROIDERY, Effie Mitrofanis
CUTWORK, HEDEBO & BRODERIE ANGLAISE, ed Jules & Kaethe Kliot
TRADITIONAL DESIGNS IN HARDANGER EMBROIDERY, ed. Jules & Kaethe Kliot
THE ART OF SHETLAND LACE, Sarah Don
CREATING ORIGINAL HAND-KNITTED LACE, Margaret Stove
THE KNITTED LACE PATTERNS OF CHRISTINE DUCHROW V I-III. ed. Kliot
BERLIN WORK, SAMPLERS & EMBROIDERY OF THE 19TH C. Raffaella Serena
THE MAGIC OF FREE MACHINE EMBROIDERY, Doreen Curran
DESIGNS FOR CHURCH EMBROIDERIES, Thomas Brown & Son
EMBROIDERY WITH BEADS, Angela Thompson
BEAD WORK, ed. by Jules & Kaethe Kliot
BEAD EMBROIDERY, Joan Edwards
BEAD EMBROIDERY, Valerie Campbell-Harding and Pamela Watts
INNOVATIVE BEADED JEWELRY TECHNIQUES, Gineke Root
BEADED ANIMALS IN JEWELRY, Letty Lammens and Els Scholte
CLASSIC BEADED PURSE PATTERNS, E. de Jong-Kramer
CREATIVE LOCKER HOOKING, Leone Peguero
THE ART OF NETTING, ed. Jules & Kaethe Kliot
TENERIFFE LACE, ed. Jules & Kaethe Kliot
THE BARGELLO BOOK, Frances Salter
FLORENTINE EMBROIDERY, Barbara Muller

For a complete list of LACIS titles, write to:

LACIS

3163 Adeline Street, Berkeley, CA 94703 US